Alternatives!
A Memoir

Sustainability and More Community Fun in Just 10% of Our Time

Chapters from the life of a slightly adventurous woman as she becomes an environmental activist.

Paula Morrow

Cover photos
1) 1971 by Steven Creagh
Paula Bellmaine, (first married name then) later Morrow (from 2nd marriage) and son Carlos at commune in Yandina, South East Queensland

2) 2017 by Alex Bainbridge
Paula Morrow arrested protesting against the Adani mine up near Bowen on the Adani private road very near the port and very near the Great Barrier Reef

Copyright © Paula Morrow 2021

Many thanks to the early readers of this manuscript: Sally Fitzpatrick, Paul Skye and John Ward. Also to writers' group friends Luke Kendall and Barbara Strickland for encouragement near the finish.

Many thanks to Abigail Morrow and Alexander Provost for help with cover design and text formatting.

Published by Tomorrow Publications
10/109 Lawson St Hamilton, 2303
Australia
Webpage: paulamorrow.net

ISBN: 978-0-9807426-3-3

Contents

Introduction	7
The Overland Trip – from Australia to London	9
Looking Back from the Nineties	10
The Patris	12
To Ceylon	13
To India	18
To Nepal	28
To Pakistan	36
Iran	41
Kuwait	44
Greece, the Destination!	56
Germany	65
Vilification Unhelpful in Lockout Debate	72
Flashback to some of my earliest influences	75
London	78
Paris January 1968	84
Back in London	86
Going Home	91
Goodbye to Paula and Peter a poem by Paul Delofski	94
A Note	97
Fun in the Sun	98
Houses	102
FIRE	103
The Bust	105

Mullumbimby Dreaming	109
Love One Another RIGHT NOW	112
A Review of the movie *Kokoda* by Paula Morrow 2006	127
Saving the figs, or not. 2011	133
Oh Newcastle! Oh Planet! a poem	140
The Joy of Protest 2015	143
Broughton Hall 1963 - Flashback	150
Moods, Food Cravings, Addictions: notes for workshop August 2017	154
Three Elders and a Television Set.	157
The Arrest! What is a conservationist these days?	160
Chat with Eva, the shuttle-car driver in Bowen 2017	179

List of Photos

Photo 1 The Patris, 1965	9
Photo 2 Quetta early 1966	40
Photo 3 Restaurant/Bar, Munich 1966	71
Photo 4 Anti-Vietnam-War Protest, London 1968	89
Photo 5 The Shota Rustaveli 1968	93
Photo 6 Banana Shed, Yandina Commune 1971	108
Photo 7 The Aquarius Festival, Nimbin 1973	126
Photo 8 The Florentine, Tasmania 2007	149
Photo 9 Police across road, anti-Adani arrests 2017	181
Photo 10 Outside court after appearing Oct 2017	182
Photo 11 Carlos's 50th birthday 2018	183

Dedication:

To my children.

To my grandchildren and step-grandchildren.

To my nephews.

To my honorary nieces and nephews and those by marriage.

To all the children of the world.

Introduction

We can look back at our lives through a lot of themes I suppose. I had never felt that particularly.

Until giving a talk on Sustainability and Protest in Tasmania when I had to think of my history in both those fields.

Until the Gloucester talk I gave at their Sustainability Festival when I saw it in a broader way; it had been a life of involvement in Alternative Living projects.

Until giving a Writer's Talk at Newcastle University when the Law Department ran a *Narratives of Climate Change Symposium* in 2018 when it became really clear that my life and the books I have written are a path looking at better ways..

From the very early and extended backpacking travel from Australia, then overland from Ceylon through 26 countries to London.

From living on probably the first commune of the modern era in Australia.

Between the camping in the showground, as part of the protest against AGL mining wanting to mine coal, and the going back there to give a talk as part of their Sustainability Festival.

My second husband and I studied a lot of conventional Medicine as well as Natural Therapies and we tried to grow food and herbs organically.

By the 1980s I realised that you have to have healthy soil, air and water to grow food and medicine for people.

I started joining in with the environmental movement.

That is the theme I am following in this memoir.

Before

Perhaps it was the silken breeze,

that took the collective mind back?

Back to the impossible friendships

of childhood and youth.

Such love they had for that friend,

that long lost friend.

That friend they had betrayed.

When hearts were still whole.

The Overland Trip – from Australia to London

Getting Away

The Patris carried us away from Australia to the world when we were nineteen. The huge need I had for adventure, for synthesis, was about to be realised in a number of smaller adventures and the shock of the old and of how the world is, or how it was and still is, in the only slowly-changing places. On the Patris we were on the beginning of the wave that took us, me at least open-mouthed, through 26 countries and three years and where I found myself working as a film extra in Bombay, selling my blood and whisky in Kuwait, being a waitress in Athens, working for the BBC in London, and through the birth of a son.

Photo 1 The Patris, 1965

Looking Back from the Nineties

I am afraid that we are all in danger of becoming embittered, for different reasons. So I am thinking back to when we first met.

Even when we were all very young, just turning eighteen, Julian had a highly developed sense of the aesthetics of dress and behaviour.

'Look, I smoke Dunhill for the sake of the look of the packet in the front pocket as much as for any other reason of preference,' he said.

I vaguely realised then, the extent of our differences in outlook. I rolled my own. Drum. Perhaps playing to a different gallery.

I remember the Dunhill conversation from so many years ago at a pub in Milson's Point where I played Ray Charles often on the juke box. Especially 'Lucky Old Sun' which expressed a curious mixture of blues and fate, bad luck and good luck and alcohol.

It was 1965. The year that Peter and I sailed on the Patris for Columbo and the overland trip. I had never heard of anyone else doing it. Just looked at the map and thought what a lot of land you miss going by boat or air straight to Europe.

Greece was the envisaged destination, because of Lawrence Durrell. And because of Zorba.

Peter and I quoted the movie to each other often, especially 'Wife! Children! Mortgage! The Full Catastrophe!'

Someone lent us 'Dust On My Shoes' by the Australian Peter Pinney. I think it was probably Julian, he has always had the most books and called them his 'library'. But I read at least as many. I read it just before we left. Pinney had gone a similar route: some of the way by elephant.

We worked at two jobs for six months to save the fare to go. In the daytime I soldered switchboards in a factory in North Sydney. From the window I could see the office building I had to clean at night.

Peter and I still found time for drinking; often with Julian and sometimes with the sweet and elegant Sallie who was doing Arts at Sydney Uni. Where I should have been. We frequented pubs in Milson's Point or North Sydney and sometimes continued in our bedsitter tucked behind Luna Park which was then happily neon-ed and noisy most of the night but it didn't worry us. Julian tried to talk us into painting the walls of our tiny place a better colour even though we were leaving Australia in only two weeks. He was a dress designer then but had not yet given up on the idea of becoming a artist.

We were all eighteen and in love.

After a night of too much beer, I'd wake up faint and sick, and trembling outside to the bathroom, stumble past a huge mound of beer bottles propped up against the grey fibro of the outside of the building. On the better nights that's where the bottles would end up, anyhow. But after I'd made a cup of tea, and rolled and lit a cigarette in the tiny kitchenette, I'd inhale the view of the daylight-silenced big dipper and the bit of dirty harbour, and the potential day seemed liveable after all.

The Patris

Leaving Sydney Harbour on a big ship was the most exhilarating moment of my nineteen years. I was in rapture at being on board, and with a hand on the big timber banisters, just floated down the wide timber staircases to the little cabin down low. The smell of wood and salt and engine oil and the fluttering streamers. It was our day. Bigger than any wedding. But when we and our little group were standing around, in one of the staterooms, looking out to the dock and the water on only three sides still, saying goodbye and I was holding flowers, Grandma cried and said she'd never see me again. Papa shushed her. I adored them. They both died in the three years we were away.

The streamers broke.

The voyage was better than Kings Cross and Manly beach rolled together. Three course Greek meals twice a day. I ate octopus for the first time. Friendly Greek waiters kept bringing more seafood and fluffy rice and exotic vegetables. After so much work: no work, bars, cafes, card-playing and a swimming pool.

To be on the sea, far away from any land. Affected every minute by the sky and the water. All was mostly blue, benign and beneficent. But when the sky was grey, the swollen sea menaced; the huge ship felt very small, and fell about, and the hospitable table settings slid noisily around in the deserted dining-room.

When the weather blessed us again, late at night up on the bow deck, under beckoning stars, homeward-bound Greeks would dance their dances culminating in the 'hoppa!' which conveyed to me their ecstasy at being alive and together and heading home. The Mediterranean beckoned them, and us.

To Ceylon

The Patris was the ship that took us away to the world. The first officer on the Patris was called Yuri and when I exclaimed over that name because it was only lately that a Yuri Gagarin had been the first person in space, he said that he was half-Russian. I was excited by anything Russian in those days because of Dostoevsky, because of The Brothers Karamazov in fact, as well as by everything Greek because of Zorba. (It's funny now it's everything Italian that tickles most people's brains lately in that way and means wine and dancing, means culture, romance. Means leisure, funny how we get re-programmed, or re-program ourselves, re-program the bio-computer.)

Yuri was very attractive with dark knock-out sort of good looks and very dark eyes which he fixed on you while standing really close and bending forward attentively so his face was only about six inches from yours. He always wore the white officer's uniform with its brass buttons and although I had deliberately tried to make myself immune to any sex appeal due to money, I had not yet had much experience with that associated with power. I mean 1st officer not 17th.

I vaguely wondered why he championed us but I suppose that we were attractive too, I was slim and spirited and had the long blond hair. Peter was young and handsome, talented and witty.

Yuri had a sister called Sophie in Athens. Peter and I were to meet her later and we three went out with a guy called Socrates! and compromised ourselves drinking in The Plaka. There in the most sophisticated part of Athens it transpired that she was thought of as like a prostitute because she was divorced and dyed her hair! But we were not in Greece yet.

Yuri was aghast that we were getting off in Colombo. He continually travelled the world and he said that no-one got off in Colombo. He offered to smuggle us to Greece in his cabin. I wondered if the cabin could possibly be big enough that the offer could be without attached strings. I only wondered this in a subconscious sort of way. It's only now that I am older that those issues always stare me hard in the face. I had never seen his cabin and didn't want to.

I was only a few months married and though Peter hadn't been the first I was sort of fiercely married, had placed all my emotional eggs in one basket, a basket that was to prove to last only seven years. Still seven years, if it had been seven months my vulnerable mental state might have gone under again. I might have believed I was a slut. Such a lot of my feeling bad has always been to do with the difficulty in being an angel. The legacy from my family was we have to be totally morally upright but sorry there's no spiritual reality, no rewards. So I didn't want to explore Yuri's officer cabin and sleeping arrangements and anyway we were committed to going overland from Colombo. But nice to be asked, would his job have been on the line?

Colombo was all that Yuri had feared. The smell of rotting vegetables through the sweating heat hit the nose like a mushy fist. There was plenty of concrete so I recognised it as a city. Concrete holds back the jungle. The beggars in the streets caused the mind shock. I particularly noticed a large man who had a habit of thrusting his leprous-looking arm in my face. My first experience of people who spent all day on the footpath begging. And they are not polite about it. Shouldn't distress be hidden?

The people are attractive, small and brown and lithe, they have the suppleness born of using the body, of sensing the body. The saris are in jewel colours: ruby, emerald, lapis lazuli, turquoise, with silver borders. Peacock colours! And fruit colours! Orange, lemon. We didn't have those extreme and joyous colours for some reason in Aus, unless very occasionally, at night-time celebrations, in the theatre perhaps, or at the Manly Mardi Gras. Extravagant colours, colours you could lose yourself in. And the Ceylonese men just in white or brown. Like birds but turned around. At last I knew what sensual meant.

But the saris of the very poor have lost their colour.

The food burnt our mouths out!

Someone advised us to stay in the Sailors' Home which sounded unlikely but we went there and yes we could have a room. It seemed to be more guest house than nautical and there we first met the tall old ceilings and the big soothing ceiling fans that spelled Ceylon and India. That spell a little cool breeze for the Caucasian who was born elsewhere and really has no business there I suppose.

We went for a four-day jeep trip into the countryside: fecund dense tangled and deep tropical green. We had dinner at a hospitable family's. I tried one mouthful and was then in serious pain and ran to the toilet, trying to regain my breath.

And we stayed by the coast one night in a rest house, another sign of the Raj. A simple building, mosquito nets, and from outside over the darkening water there was a distant fishing boat with just a triangular rough thick sail made perhaps of bark. On the grey evening sea, with the light and pink in the sky. That sail creaked open some awareness within me. Such power in an age-old shape and symbol. I was aware of the countless years of fishing, of heartache, of beauty.

I can number on my two hands the occasions when a vision such as that sail has picked me up and spun me around to see things skewed right skewed important skewed meaningful I suppose.

I was stuck writing poems about futility when I was seventeen.

> *Our world,*
>
> *just an ugly misshapen marble,*
>
> *tossed out of a giants' game.*

And I don't mean that other precious way of seeing, when you look down your dusty street one evening and it is transformed – those experiences make things totter momentarily – etch the month differently.

But those rare and stronger images knock significance in to hard heads. I think they were what I was looking for in all my drug experiences. With LSD I got something like that but only really the first time. The time that I had it mixed with methedrine and injected by a psychiatrist friend.

Later I felt that same shifting of the reality plates with the birth of each child.

And later still when my second husband died, unafraid at the age of thirty-five. Leaving us. I felt that crack open between the worlds again, felt the draught upon my own self but was left again with sweetness and trembling from contact with the other side, just the same as with birth. And all I could do, the only existential response, was a poem.

Now the next moon.

Also a sweet smile.

But the guardian star has slipped

a little,

over the running tide.

But when I was nineteen and in Ceylon, I had just come from a place where everything was new, where only the new was appreciated.

I had no idea of the old.

To India

From Colombo we went by ship to India. It just took overnight but it was rough and I was sick. My love for boats and ships was not extending to rough water. We climbed down from the small ship onto smaller boats, crowded together with dark-skinned people. We all had baggage and parcels held tightly as we out-boarded it to India. There was a large shed for the desultory customs activity. It was hot and the sky was very large and I remember even it as pale brown like the earth beneath it. There were only a few people about and they looked much as they did in Ceylon. I was aware of the openness of the world and my going into it in this way.

In Madras we somehow ended up staying in the home of a Catholic priest. I was offered a small room in the morning for bathing. There was a metal bucket about a third full of cold water and a hole in the floor toilet. That bathroom which befuddled me at first was to be luxury compared to what was coming. I was to meet many of those and be glad to – they were better than the alternative, nothing, people just eliminating on the ground, even close to densely populated areas.

Madras is known for its extremely hot curries. We had serious hunger problems. Curry was all there was, anywhere. There were lots of people in the dusty roads. There was a group around a man whistling up a snake out of a basket. With an eerie little tune out of a tiny sort of recorder thing. And the cobra swayed up to greet him, and to be admired. The audience was mostly men and boys in white dhotis, simple cloths neatly wrapped. They watched quietly, seriously. I thought this actually happens still? Although

I recognised this scene somehow, I knew that such experiences existed in the past, and in books and films, but here, in actuality? In my modern world!

(An early indication, that although I was sort of educated and came from a progressive, social-justice-minded family, I was (as my whole country was and is) very parochial, ie blinkered. This was to even put my life at risk.)

We caught the train to Bombay. At every station there were people who sold food. The sellers didn't usually have much English but they smiled with great enthusiasm and waved things at us through the train windows. Everything, even little patties: cakes I hoped, turned out to be little fireworks that exploded chilli needles into our soft virgin mouths.

Nothing was bland about India. Blandness had been left behind in the suburbs of Sydney. Tiny bananas were often sold and we ate them. Somewhere along the way, when the train stopped long enough, we found that fried eggs were sold. They became the staple along with bananas.

At home Grandma had occasionally cooked 'curry' and it had hardly had any taste at all except sweet and salty and certainly no heat. Australia in 1965 had yet to be touched by Italian food, French food, Indian food let alone Thai or Vietnamese food.

I actually dreamed of steak and vegetables once in Bombay, just grilled steak, tomato sauce, mashed potato and peas. I woke up very hungry. We managed to have that sort of food once or twice, in expensive restaurants. Without the tomato sauce, and the potatoes and peas were lightly curried not mashed. We were culturally, geographically and gastronomically adrift.

We found a couple of cafes in Bombay whose fried eggs we

could eat. Sometimes they were swimming in oil. We drank the sweet cups of chai. We smoked and all of a sudden we were smoking funny brands from anywhere, British Virginia things, as well as the American ones we were used to.

People smoked bidis and chewed betel nut. So as well as the exotic sounds and colours and advanced designs on material everywhere and the various spices and curries that started to smell wonderful long before they tasted wonderful, there was the special bidi smell and the sight of red stained mouths and footpaths, did I say footpaths? Ground I should say, dusty paths made only by feet, stained red from the spat-out betel-nut. Splattered like blood.

On one train trip in India we were sitting on seats all around the edges of a carriage. This was unusual. Both the arrangements of the seats and the fact that we found some to sit on. We were travelling 4th class and usually could only sit on the floor with most of the other occupants. On longer trips I had slept on the floor under the seats. One time our simple camera was stolen from around my neck while I was doing that. I'd also slept high up on luggage racks and they were relatively comfortable and out of the reach of inquisitive hands.

Anyway, when we were all sitting around facing each other that day, a young woman beggar got on with a very small child, he must have been about 2 years old and as she pulled him onto the train, he hurt his shins on the stairs. She held his hand firmly and he cried a little as they went around while she held out her hand to each person in the carriage. Quite a few people handed her a coin, as always in India. They don't have the 'mustn't encourage' reaction like in the West. I find it funny that in the US of A. people seem to think that if you bring in for example health insurance, you will attack the very root of human endeavour. A terror of the collective.

But very small coins. When they got to us, the baby put his head on my knees in exhaustion. I was stricken with tenderness like a blow. I touched his tiny trusting head. To see a baby in despair. How could I have lived 19 years and not known how it is for people? Although I did in the psych hospital I worked in at 17. Thoughts of rescue.

I gave him an awkward pat; other people gave me sympathetic looks as if this was a rending of the rules. We gave a tiny coin too, and they got off. It was the start of my real education.

We remained in India, mainly in Bombay, for three months. Luckily we got jobs as film extras. We didn't mean to stay that long but India and Pakistan were at war. The border between them was closed. Bombay was under blackout. This only added to the exotic effect which was extreme already. The discordant sound of Indian music, the always shuffling, murmuring crowds, bright beautiful designs on material everywhere, not only on the women, but hanging and billowing in the wind off stalls and drying off buildings.

People treated us well and were usually very interested in us, often crowding around us and staring. The ones with English would question us and translate for the others.

One day a couple of young Indian men asked us to come to a café they knew for a cup of chai. We went through a maze of tiny lanes to find the place. The café, as often, was just a hole in a wall of a building and the tables and chairs were in the lane with some material slung over as a shelter from the sun.

One of the guys rolled a joint and we thought hooray, the first since we left home. It was passed around and Peter and I inhaled deeply. It went around once, then again, the next thing I knew was a sort of swooning into unconsciousness interrupted by a crash which was Peter falling to the ground and which had the effect of galvanising me awake and terrified. The men were laughing! I started screaming and a Sikh, a turbaned Indian man came running up the lane in response. He helped me drag the groggy Peter to his feet. One of the laughing men called out 'come back and have cocaine with me tomorrow, blond girl'.

With Peter supported between us the Sikh led us back through the maze to the main street. 'Never go in those places,' he said. 'You were in big danger'.

Peter was fine by then and didn't seem to even think that it had been a big deal. But I was in a panic and it continued even though we got back safely to our hotel room. It was a basic and nasty room, three single beds with bare and dirty mattresses. A room we shared with another young traveller to save money. He was there, and Peter and he chatted about the event and smoked, and I lay on my back with a racing heart for the entire afternoon. Whether it was a drug effect or whether it was the realisation of my vulnerability, my body admitting for once how little it would take to die, or to find life physically unbearable, I couldn't tell.

The only other thing I remember of that hotel room, was that out the window on some lower roofs, many cats roamed. They were twice as big as the ones in my country, and I watched them and wondered about such big cats, in a country of small and thin people. And whether they could be a cross between cats and tigers though they were the usual catty colours. I had yet to meet the cows. There was a bit of greenery, it looked like weeds around the outbuildings there. The only thing remnant green I ever saw in the enormous inner-city of Bombay.

Oh yes and I had fear like that in Kuwait too. But we're not there yet.

The Salvation Army hostel was where we ended up staying in Bombay, after the filthy cheap hotels that we couldn't afford. A wooden multi-storeyed place with verandas on every level where we could meet the other inhabitants to play cards and swap survival stories. The dining room offered corned beef with boiled potatoes, white sauce. Wonderful blandness, served by uncommunicative and perhaps disapproving Christians. We could only afford their meals sometimes but we were thankful.

We played cards and swapped stories with an American couple. He was white and cool. Zita was very black and her pink tongue and mouth were like an exclamation mark. I'd never seen a black person before. There was Black Alan who played the guitar in the Royal George in Sydney and we'd had aboriginal friends in Cairns, in the hitch-hiking around Australia bit. They'd saved us from police harassment, by harassing the police back actually. They called themselves black, but they were all definitely brown in comparison with Zita.

I always liked cards. From building houses with them on the carpet as a solitary child, to euchre with my grandfather to rummy with the surf club boys. We played poker and blackjack with Dave and Zita, way into the nights. Scary games. Games where you can lose all your money in one afternoon and we were to do just that further on in Athens.

Even later we could hear the streetwise couple yelling at one another through the thin wooden walls of the bedrooms. She seemed so distraught; she screamed with an absolute anger and despair. I thought it might have something to do with the dangerous difference in the colours of their skin. Everyone gaped at them, even this far from the savage history of their homeland. They were always fine in the daytime.

Bombay was swollen with people. Five hundred thousand slept on the streets, the shop awnings their only shelter. Whole families, some had little businesses selling leather thonged sandals, more ornate than the Australian rubber variety, or just individual cigarettes. They had tiny fuel stoves and perhaps a 24-hour tenancy. Others just slept and moved on in the morning. Such a long day in that heat, with nowhere comfortable to rest, nowhere to be at home.

We met some clerks when we were trying to get some documentation. They had so little room in the flimsy wooden offices they shared but they had white-collar dignity. Perhaps they slept on the streets too. The reality we had known nothing of before, that in the real world, you are either lucky and have a way to make a living, or you struggle to stay alive probably in continual pain and suffering.

But the Indians had such vitality. I think they live more in the body. They are a great advertisement for yoga even if they don't do any.

People had such spirit, and such enthusiastic interest in us. We met a young boy who worked behind a little stall ironing items for a tiny fee. We had a couple of things ironed by him occasionally.

Fancy taking clothes that needed ironing on a trip like that! After the first few countries we gave up on that. I had a short sleeveless cotton dress with bright blobs of orange and purple flowers with green on a white background. My Mum made it for me. And Peter had a long-sleeved shirt with a thin brown stripe in it. Those were the things that we initially tried to get ironed. I had a synthetic dress as well. I carried what would today be thought of as a very small backpack and a small overnight bag. I had three pairs of shoes: two of them with small heels on them, one pair junior navy and the other shocking pink. I carried them a long way and then somehow left them behind in Greece by mistake. I felt quite a sense of loss. Those remnants of a previous life in Sydney. I did have some black flatties too and wore them the whole time.

When we were leaving Bombay to go to Kathmandu, we said goodbye to the little ironing boy, he couldn't have been more than 10, all we could think of to give him was a pair of cheap sunglasses. He put them on and pranced around turning his ironing cubby hole into theatre. We saw him later in the street and still his walk spelt new sunglasses.

It took me years to understand the difference in world view that different cultures have. It put my life at risk in Arabia; not understanding these things. I thought I was cool but I was locked into my world view even though I had a great curiosity and openness. We were insular for a long time after we thought we were citizens of the world.

Years later I studied Cultural Relativity in Philosophy. It should be taught in schools.

I started to love curry eventually. I first liked a dry fish curry from the canteen sort of thing on the movie lot where we were working as film extras.

There was a tall young Indian man with westernised manners – what do I mean by that? emotions hidden? clamped down? He came soliciting for Europeans to work as film extras and found us on the veranda of the Salvation Army place. He offered us 30 rupees a week plus lunch which started out as sandwiches; he knew about Europeans. This probably saved us from starvation as our money was getting low and there was no sign of the end of the war between India and Pakistan.

There followed long days on sets. We mostly sat around, and I either watched the fantastic Indian dance scenes, the women using their whole bodies, especially their hands, fabulous posture, dark hair swaying, the spot on the forehead, the saris luscious, often in blues every shade to turquoise and silver in the material and on the many-bangled arms. Then at some point in every movie they had a party scene and they apparently needed Europeans in those. So we and a few other well-worn travellers would brandish our glasses of coke that were supposed to be spirits, and talk and look like what they wanted, sophisticated and urbane, jetsetters or at least trendsetters – us in our many-times washed clothes.

I read Catch 22 on those sets and loved it. Later I wanted to call my first-born Yossarian but knew people would respond with 'what sort of a hell name is that?' and settled for Carlos. These days I wish that I had read some Indian history or something while I was there. Or some background to Hinduism to cast light on the holy pictures and sculptured many-limbed Kalis and others everywhere around us.

For some reason sandwiches weren't available one day on the set and we found ourselves down at the canteen staffed and frequented by the crowds of Indians connected with the filming. They had little dried looking fish that I knew would have some curry involvement but someone urged me to try one and I ate it with some rice and a chapatti and it tasted good! Only a little sting in the mouth and worth it! Better than the sandwiches!

I then found the curry that was served on some trains. I only remember eating on trains a couple of times, we mustn't have been travelling 4th class those times. The joy of the stainless-steel trays with the little separate bowls set in so it wouldn't spill. You could have a bit of this and a bit of that being very careful to isolate the most outrageous chilli ones.

By the time I left those countries where they eat with their fingers, I was used to it and strangely then found it a sensory deprivation to leave it behind. I missed the licking of fingers, the fingers in the food and in my mouth, the wiping the plate with chapatti. We went forward, or backward to cold, metal knives and forks in our soft mouths.

To Nepal

You would think that India would not be a good country to get toothache in and you would be right. I had a shocking, mental-making toothache there, but I went to a dentist who treated me and then said he wouldn't charge me because I was a traveller and I had made the effort to come to his country.

Nice, this approach to travellers as being in some way special. Better than the hitch-hiking around Australia and therefore being branded slut by heavy, unrestrained cops, and the 'summary offences act' which saw me thrown into gaol more than once, for vagrancy, for having 'no visible means of support.' Hopefully in these welfare days, that exact crime can no longer exist.

There were Sikh temples dotted all around India and in those any travellers could sleep for up to three nights for nothing. Just floor space but that was a luxury. We stayed in a big city one in Bombay for the allotted three nights. It had tall ceilings and wall hangings and rugs on the floor, and many people slept all in the one room, from there we went each morning to the central railway station and paid for showers.

In New Delhi the Sikh temple was new and it had small rooms with polished board floors and although there were just the two of us in one of those rooms the floor felt very hard and it somehow wasn't as comfy or comforting as sleeping in the immense peopled, cave-like one before.

Holy men, and perhaps women now? roamed the country hopefully thinking themselves to enlightenment, and like the Buddhist monks elsewhere, didn't waste their precious spiritual resources on thoughts of making a living. Travelling does of necessity entail non-attachment, the beginning point for active religions like Buddhism.

And Mother Theresa has said, 'at least the poor are lucky in one thing, they have time to think about god'. It may be particularly the Hindu and the Buddhist faiths that see the wandering, vagrant life as having purpose and value, even though Christ, too, said 'consider the lilies of the field...'

I was brought up in that atheist household to think that people in countries such as India were deliberately tricked into religions so that they wouldn't rebel about their unfortunate conditions on earth. And they were very sincere about the atheism, brought about by my wonderful grandfather's disavowal of the Christianity he had taken very seriously before he found himself in the trenches of France in the First World War. He'd gone as a stretcher-bearer because he'd refused 'to carry a gun' and he'd decided out there, that there mustn't be a god because God wouldn't let men do that to one another.

The wrong question I would say now. The right one as far as ethics and conscience go but the wrong conclusion as to what a spiritual life should be limited by. I have thought about this all my life Papa, and studied Philosophy to see if the possibilities of spiritual realities are ruled out in Philosophy or by Science. I love these latter but found that no, they don't rule out the other possibilities of spiritual realities or experiential religion: as long as those things don't harm others....

So after the war Papa joined the communist party. Idealists must have something to believe in. I can remember the reverberations in the household when 'Stalin walked into Hungary' as Grandma told it to me. I was about ten and when I got home from school, the shockwaves were as if there had been a death in the family.

So Papa left the communist party. He did me the very great favour of, from the time I was about twelve, engaging me in conversation about the state of the world, dinner was often eaten amid hypothetical arguments between the capitalist and communist ideologies. My mother and grandmother were much more passive although mum was interested. They would just tend to say 'don't be rude to your grandfather!' if I got a bit vehement. But he would just say 'it's good for the girl to think'. He had no great need to win these arguments. My life with the three of them was quite good there for a while. But it was there that I had the shock of hearing about Hiroshima.

The toothache unfortunately flared up again on the way to Nepal. The word had gone around among the very few European travellers in Ceylon and India 'go to Kathmandu for Christmas'. We were on a bus on the last leg of the journey to Raxaul which is the border-town between India and Nepal, when the whole side of my face swelled up to be level with my nose and red-hot, rigid and agonising.

We got off the bus and people could see the searing pain. They didn't need English to direct us to a small hospital run by nuns, both western and Indian. They were so gentle and caring to us. Another example of people not assuming that wanderers were bad? They made us sit down on chairs in a quiet room and brought us tea and toast and marmalade! on a tray – don't believe it when they tell you there was nothing good about the Raj! An older English woman dressed in a brown nun's habit was very encouraging to me and a younger Indian nurse in an immaculate starched uniform gave me a shot in the bum with a big syringe of penicillin. There was no censure there. They would take no payment and sent us on our way with a jar of penicillin tablets and it worked. Over the next twenty-four hours, the face went down and the pain ebbed away.

Just as well really because the next night we ate in a café, part way into Nepal, where there was snow on the ground but the people were still walking around barefoot. We ate the dhal and rice with need and pleasure, and about then I realised how it keeps half the world alive. After we ate, tables were pushed back and it was indicated that we should go to sleep on the mud floor because our truck driver for the trip through the Himalayas to Kathmandu wouldn't arrive for us until 4am.

It was hard to sleep but harder to wake up on the cold floor. We gathered ourselves and climbed into the truck with a Nepalese driver who spoke no English and another man who spoke a little.

We drove without speaking through the black and cold. There was no room to pass. Occasionally we came upon someone going the other way and both drivers would brake and one would back up and they would then sidle around each other. As it started to get light I could see immense drops right beside us. This was alarming coupled with the driving style, fast between corners which came upon us every second, then slam on the brakes and edge around. There were signs written in Nepalese at intervals too and when I asked what they said we were told 'No travelling at night, Danger, Landslides'. Just when I was most frightened the freezing light started to show, over the drops, on the other sides of the valley, mountains terraced, and as the eye followed them up, snow and ice went up and up to pinnacles way above, and all around us. And as the sky showed its blue between them and beyond them, the peaks and the snow blankets turned pink, pale orange, pink and clouds moved above adding their reflections. We were immersed in sunrise on snow, in a vertical landscape.

I'd only seen snow once before, at Mount Kosciusko when I was seventeen, on a not-planned car trip with other psyche nurses at the end of a night drinking. I remember my hands hurt so much from the cold and I slid around on dirty ice.

We were not dressed properly in Nepal either, just jeans and jumper, I was glad that the four of us were squashed together in the front of the little old truck. Body warmth, is it all we can rely on?

In shock at the grandeur. The overwhelming silent colour dialogue of the white mountains with sky.

I hung on mentally for hours, rushing into corners and stopping as we hit them, loving the vistas, promising myself that if there was any other way out again, we would take it. Hanging on, just to my inner self, possessing nothing more substantial, knowing the danger.

Kathmandu, the word must be one of the most beautiful and evocative in itself for any world place. There are a few that work for me like that. Kathmandu, Quetta, Kabul, Istanbul. No, there are many. I look at the map of India and surrounds now, I didn't look at it then, and I see names, places we went to and ones I only heard about and beautiful ringing names are everywhere, Amritsar, Kundahar, Benares, Srinagar, Kashmir, Islamabad.

They say Sanskrit is a divinely revealed language.

In Kathmandu we stayed in dormitory-style accommodation

above a Tibetan café. I remember the smell and taste of the yummy broiled meat that permeated upstairs, I can taste it today in its rich tasting gravy with a wild sort of edge to it, was it yak?

There was also an open air toilet inside, downstairs, the sort you would only get way down the backyard in Australia, in my childhood I occasionally met one of those, or today in isolated camping grounds but never so over-used. One toilet for the dormitory that slept about 20, and for the café and the family who ran them both as well. I remember it as the scene of the worst diarrhoea of my life. The sort that leaves you shaky and sweating and wondering if you'll lose your actual insides to this stinking place, or even fall right in out of weakness. Such a disgusting little room of pain and fear in this magic far-away place?

When we walked into the market in Kathmandu, it had some sort of cover high up, and the light that drifted in and around was gentle and dreamlike, it felt unchanged since medieval times. I felt rocked by seeing it, greatly privileged, like peeping and tiptoeing back into time. I only went once, and I didn't stay long, I didn't want to affect it, like a secret place. I felt this place has been here, with people merchandising like this for at least a thousand years. It seemed to me that faces looked vaguely up at me from their business, not fully focussed, and I was from the distant future.

We met a Swiss guy called Fred, just a few years older than us in the Tibetan doss house. He read us Krishnamurti aloud, and he lent him to me to read as well. Which I did, sitting on the stretcher bed that was one of about twelve on this floor. Fred was tall and fair with a moustache; he was a bit older than us. That probably made him late twenties. Fred was one of the two men I met on that long journey whom I could have fallen for. A singular person on a wisdom search. It seemed to me that Fred (as well as Krishnamurti) was trying to come to enlightenment via an intellectual leap, without the obfuscations of religion.

That should have served me well but Krishnamurti didn't really turn me on. Fred could have though. Look I say that now, (in about the year 2003) I wouldn't have allowed myself to even think it then. He wondered if we might like to go with him to a meeting he had set up with the Dalai Lama. Sadly we somehow didn't feel up to that, suddenly shy and inadequate. I didn't feel enough substance, not knowing then that most people who meet the Dalai Lama are nowhere in his league.

We stayed about two weeks in Kathmandu, away from the Indian heat and flurry of people. We could sometimes get a small pan of warm water from the kitchen if we asked when they were not too busy. There was a tiny room to bathe in. Once I bent and washed my long hair under the tap out in the street and immediately felt the mistake in that – shocked by the freezing water! In that ancient street, cobble stones, two storey simple dwellings, small windows, did they watch the stranger at the tap?

The Nepalese seemed more self-contained than the Indians had been. Than the Indians of the hot low country anyway, the only ones we had met. And the Tibetans, the refugees, of the wide and beautiful faces, of the dark hair and red cheeks, such rosy cheeks as I was only to see once again, in Persia. Neither people as curious about us as the Indians always were. Better for them I think.

We walked up to Nagacote, a day's outing, up those steep tracks, where Nepalese overtook us regularly, walked right past us, even though burdened by huge loads of firewood on their backs. We could see Everest from there, just another snow-covered giant marching with the others into the distance, but with connotations of record and adventure that had spread even as far as the Sydney of my growing up.

There were very few vehicles registered in Nepal. A few government jeeps and diplomatic cars. A truck went over the side in the fortnight that we were in Kathmandu.

Once or twice we went to a quite luxurious hotel lounge for a drink and a look at how rich tourists might live, even in this isolated place.

We found out that yes there was a flight out to India. Planes and Boats and Trains: this was to be one of only two short plane trips in the whole long journey. It was a bit disconcerting to find, when we were waiting on the tarmac to get into the small plane that the handsome pilot was someone we had seen drinking in that fancy hotel the night before. The plane only held about twelve people. I had foolishly assumed that we would fly up and over the mountains, but we took off and headed straight at them, I noticed the locals clutching their buddhas and thought things had gone horribly wrong but then saw a way through. The plane weaved through the mountains, we were very close to the sides and twice turbulence took us frighteningly closer.

To Pakistan

We left India by boat for Pakistan on the first boat out when the Indo/Pakistani war ended and it was only a one or two night voyage but I felt instant delight at being on a small ship: the smell, the romance of ordinary living but living it on water, eating, sleeping in a bunk, on the shifting sea. When we sailed into the harbour in Pakistan on a grey day, it all thrilled me: the harbour, the surrounding land, the small boats everywhere, some bigger ones just sitting or slowly steaming up. Perhaps I understand at last, another reason my forebears migrated, a fascination with the sea! Not just the trying to get away from the mines in Cornwall, or the periodic Russian grab for territory over a Finnish Island. The poor convict bloke didn't have much choice or did he steal in order to go on a great sea adventure?

We picked up the car in Karachi.

I remember waking cramped in the tiny panel van, it wasn't long enough for me to ever straighten my legs. I crawled out of it and stood up outside, very early in the morning, feeling the emptiness of the landscape, feeling a long lonely way from anywhere. Peter was still asleep. He always insisted on having the side without the steering wheel to sleep. 'Because I'm taller.' There were about half a bucket load of tiny oranges in the car, more the colour of tangerines really. A young bloke had sold them to us the day before. They were blood-red inside and a whole world of divine orangeness in taste. Then there was some sunrise and hope in the sky.

As we drove further into the countryside towards Quetta, I

kept feeling that there was something special about the tussocky land, it even seemed to be shifting, as if the very ground itself was involved in some slow dance or dalliance.

Many years later I heard that in the nineteen thirties Quetta had been the scene of one of the most devastating earthquakes ever.

We drove into the town. It felt so far from anywhere but as we navigated the well-ordered streets we come upon a very dressed up, brass-buttoned and hard-hatted policeman! He was directing traffic on a little rotunda at a main intersection!

Quetta kept us there, having exotic and outlandish experiences for two weeks. We made what really felt like unlikely but true friendships with the local chemist, Jalal, and the photographer and the chief of police! They took us to eat at a real Chinese restaurant, dark and under-used, where we had rich-tasting meat reminiscent of the Tibetan restaurant in Kathmandu and wonderful mixed vegetables as well. I thought that perhaps we were not all that far from China.

The owners were wary, I don't know if it was because of the police chief. Our friends organised for us to stay at the house of people who were away. We had Turkish baths. We bought scarves of intricate colour and design from the markets. All the men wore them nonchalantly around their necks. There were open drains but they were properly built and neat. We walked along a street lined with drains to a little fish and chip shop once. Such luxury.

Little half inch square blocks of hash were handed to us everywhere and we ate tea and cakes in a left over so-British-cafe with big fans and high ceilings. We met and sat at a table with charming men who put their guns on the table when they sat down with us. Manners demanded that. They explained how their vendetta system worked. That if someone's uncle was murdered, they would be honour bound to kill an uncle or the equivalent in the offending family to right the family wrong, then they'd just pop over the border into Afghanistan to be immune from the police.

Jalal cried when we left. Against all odds those seemed like real friendships. We loved those three men and they loved us. I have photos of that time.

And on leaving for Afghanistan we met the customs man on the border who made us welcome in his isolated little hut and explained that in Muslim thought, Judas was swapped with Jesus at the last minute before the crucifixion and so got his.

When we came back through two weeks later there was no sign of that customs man. Or even his office. It was as if he'd been a figment of our imaginations. That info was important to me. Apparently Christianity not only still mattered to me (and I was at my furthest arc away from the spiritual) but that maybe Christ was a winner rather than a loser. I mustn't have liked that juxtaposition of good, gentle, brilliant prophet with to my young mind the most sordid defeat – crucifixion – I could imagine.

Peter and I had two bottles of whisky under the spare tyre under the car to sell. We had had three, but we had given one to the man whose family took us in, in Kabul. The family originally from Persia (I think they called it that, not Iran) who gave us the marital bed. The father cooked us wonderful big feasts including rice and meat and apricots. They had many daughters, the youngest little 4 year old round faced, rosy-cheeked, dark-haired and black eyed Mina.

Someone had suggested carrying the whisky to us way back

in a country where you were allowed to drink. (Like someone had suggested we buy a few topaz gems in Ceylon and sell them further on. The seller probably.)

Photo 2 Quetta early 1966

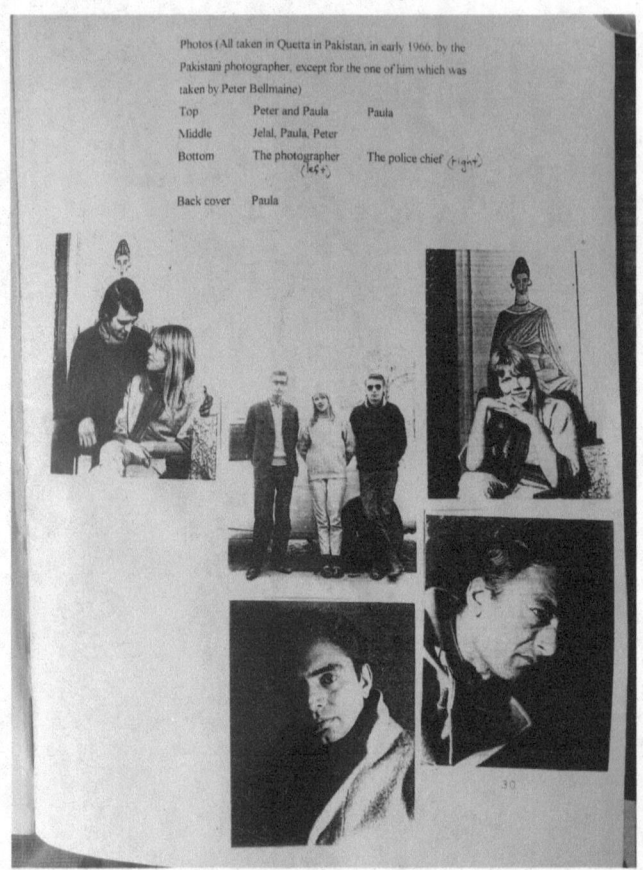

In Quetta, one of our new friends was a photographer. That's him, bottom middle. The chief of police is to his right. Top row: Peter and I. Jalal the chemist, me and Peter in the middle in front of panel-van. Me.

Iran

So now we were driving the car part of the way back to England for the young couple going the other way who had had to leave it on the Pakistan side of the Indo/Pakistan border because of the war but had somehow got through themselves.

We also carried a young family!

I haven't talked much about this huge trip over the years. Peter was to leave home when we were 24 and back in Australia with our two-year-old.

Later the second husband didn't want to hear anything much about what I did with the first!

Years later I didn't want to encourage my children towards this sort of grass-roots, dangerous travel. Frontier travel one of the two lovely sisters that I later found when I was 28, calls it.

Seeing the world at ground level might have made me much more knowledgeable and understanding of the human condition, but having the children made me much wiser. I came to see that the sort of travel I had done was partly out of an immense curiosity and sort of love for people and the world but also out of alienation, a tendency to risk-taking: almost to throwing my life away.

It was a very risk-taking trip. There were at least the two obvious times that our lives were in danger: in India, and then in Kuwait. Three: you would have to include the gun at my head at the Iran/Iraq border. And probably many others. Like I tried turning the car headlights off in Pakistan when another approached from the other direction like the truck drivers in India had done. Well, you can't see! It must have been before the time of low-beam options.

The panel-van crossing through all those countries had been hard on us. Once we had picked up the car, it was a very long way between Karachi and Greece. The huge drive across Iran, where the car made alarming noises. The only time it did anything wrong! We were forced to stop. Luckily we were coming into a settlement.

As usual, what looked like a very unpopulated sandy landscape, turned out to be lots of habitations where everyone knew each other and everyone wanted to help us. The local mechanic arrived and started work on the car at once. It turned out to be a broken engine mounting which he replaced at very little cost and off we went the next morning!

People took us to a café hidden in the landscape, like all the other simple buildings with an open oven for the flatbreads and the wonderful accoutrements!

The food was fantastic all across Iran and back before that, in India and Pakistan and Afghanistan. I was very lucky that becoming so hungry when we were caught in India with little choice, eventually forced me to try the curries, and after that, become a lot more adventurous and less fussy about food.

It was in Iran that the privations of not being able to stretch my legs at night started to hurt. The bit behind the passenger seat was not long enough to stretch out to sleep at night. Peter never let me have a turn sleeping in the longer side, I had to be squashed up behind the driver's seat which wouldn't budge, or not far, because he was taller and therefore needed the longer space more.

It made sense logically but I could have done with at least a couple of nights with my legs stretching right out on that long trip. But still we were very close through all that, it was real survival stuff, us against the world.

And we carried a little family in the back across Iran! Someone had asked us on their behalf in Pakistan whether we could give them a lift across Iran to Iraq. We had said then that we needed to sleep in the car and were told that they were happy to find somewhere to sleep every night. Which they did - possibly behind a tussock – we never saw them at night. So we had said yes.

They were so silent and clean and totally not imposing….They were a young mother and father, not much older than us and two small children.

We hardly noticed that they were in there.

But then of course, at the Iran/Iraq border, guards handed out a huge number, six or eight large capsules of some drug for each of us to take because there was a cholera epidemic somewhere ahead. I tried mildly to point out that the children should be having a lesser number of capsules because of their age.

On the basis of my one year of psyche nursing.....

And immediately had a gun put at my head.

Kuwait

Where our lives were at risk for the second or third time in the trip. That I know of!

Where Peter gets put into hospital with hepatitis.

We knew no-one in Kuwait before we got there of course: same as with every other of the 26 countries we went through or to, in this mammoth three years of travel.

We somehow got to know a Lebanese man who had a business in the main part of town and apparently had an English wife. I never met her. He was very chatty and civilised. He said that Lebanese people are not really Arabs, citing his blue eyes with a laugh and he spoke movingly about the beauty of Lebanon.

We met some young travellers. We spent at least a couple of lovely afternoons and evenings being entertained by the young Scottish singer/guitarist. *Mingulay* is the only song I remember, but I think he sang Dylan and all the great contemporaries. The popular music scene was overwhelmingly Bob Dylan and The Beatles back then. The singer was taken aback when I suggested he sing with his rich Scottish accent instead of American.

It was just Peter and I, the Scottish singer, the French guy called Patrice and the young Scottish girl and a young Canadian guy.

I got bad conjunctivitis, the worst of my life. I didn't seem to be able to find a chemist or doctor. Pus was running from my eyes in sheets and they were aching. The relief when I decided to dive into the sea! Now I think, 'God what was I wearing!'

It's the same little group of us. None of the nationals seem to swim and we don't know whether it is safe. There is evidence of some sort of metal structures in the water. But the relief of getting into the sea! I open my eyes under the water. It is a long time since I have had a swim and I am a lifelong devotee of swimming in the sea. And when I get out, my eyes are better!

(This and getting into The Dead Sea in Jordan are the only swims I can remember of the three years. And I certainly love swimming. The incredibly stimulating travel and the cultural life in London must have compensated.)

Peter suddenly seems very sick and is found to have Hepatitis and put into hospital, It must have been diagnosed within a few days of us arriving in Kuwait, otherwise I can't see that we would have planned to stay in that country for long. The Lebanese man stopped talking to us, or at least pulled right back as soon as he knew that Peter had Hepatitis. He smashed the glass I had drunk water out of in front of me when I told him the news about Peter.

Those other few travellers were all in their 20s too, except for Patrice from France who was only 18. I have just turned 20 in India and Peter won't turn 20 till August. We were the only couple I think, but I am not sure about that. When Peter was suddenly put in the hospital, I went and parked the panel van that we were driving across the world from Pakistan to Greece, outside the warehouse sort of place where the others are sleeping, and went to sleep in it.

But I wake up in the middle of the night. The van is being shaken and rocked roughly sideways backwards and forwards. I look out and there are these guys in Dhotis, you know the long white gear with head dress.

I don't know how, but luckily for me, the others inside the warehouse get involved too and it turns out that these guys, these

Kuwaitis who are, you know much older than us; maybe in their late 40s or 50s, say they want to sleep with me and the Scottish girl, otherwise we're going to jail. We say no way. And so we all end up in this Kuwaiti police station for the next sort of whatever, 14 hours was it? I don't know, but all night all morning.

My car is there although I don't remember driving it there now.

We have already heard all these scary stories about German prostitutes being murdered and buried in the sand of Kuwait and the one that says that if you go to sell your blood they will take it all from you and throw your body in the river. That sort of thing. This is the sort of thing that spreads on the rumour vines of this route, which is very sparsely travelled by Westerners back then.

So we're scared. There's a lot of silence in this police station: a lot of armed Kuwaiti guys standing around and whispering and a sense of what's to be done with us. It really, really feels scary and ominous. We are together but that is all.

I have no idea how we know, because Kuwait is just as foreign a foreign country as I ever found myself in, but we know that there is a British Consul and that because it is Saturday, it closes at 12 o'clock today.

And we decide to make a break for it. It seems insane now, and it seemed insane then, but it shows the level of our fear and desperation.

We all rush off in different directions!

I get out to the car. I drive through a first sort of little checkpoint thing and at the second one to get me out of this Police Station place, I'm stopped by a cop who puts a gun at my head.

(In my memory I have a cigarette in my hand and I attempt to burn his hand holding the gun on me, but that can't be right, can it?) (In this memoir and in my life generally, since age 17 and more and more, I try to tell the truth, it feels like my sanity depends on it.) Was I so unconsciously suicidal, even that well-coordinated? I did chain-smoke when I was young, and the more anxious I was, the more I smoked...

So that's the other time. Twice on that trip I have a gun put at my head, both by officials, totally when I'm not doing anything wrong! I still feel like crying with amazement and shock now, 54 years later. I am writing this fill-in piece from Pakistan to London now in 2020/21. I mean I am already very shocked, to have been held in this place that was totally terrifying for this night and morning.

So I'm caught and dragged back in there, and it feels really hopeless.

But then young Patrice and the Scottish singer who have also been caught and hauled back in there, tell me that the little Scottish girl and the Canadian guy have got out! They got out and they ran to a service station!

They rang and got on to the British Consul! I don't know how. Maybe there were more people speaking English in Kuwait than I remember there were. Or there was some rule of law or respect for the British still, or something. I mean it just seemed then and still seems now, so amazingly lucky! Anyway, that's about 10 to 12 or something.

The 10 minutes before the British Consul shuts for the weekend and they got through to him!

(Perhaps one of the luckiest things of my life, looking back.)

He says 'Sit tight I'll be right there!' Then you know, we are back to quaking together.

But the British Consul does come and really soon. Just a slim, 40ish Englishman in a suit. They respect him. The atmosphere changes totally and the whole terror ebbs away.

He speaks to us for a few minutes, asks us all what countries we are from and then goes and talks to the police. He does a deal with them that because Peter is in hospital I will need to stay in Kuwait, but that in exchange for that, the others can be taken to the border and put on a bus and deported. (I have a little whimper and/or laugh writing this part in 2021 - the friends - the lifeline leaving!) and that transpires.

Anyway, we were lucky! I mean we were so lucky to get the Consul even though he treated us very disdainfully, we were obviously below him or something. He says that he is not really responsible for Patrice, the French boy, but that he will lump him in with the rest of us.

He thought we were I don't know what he thought of us but we were honourable all of us. Just the first wave of backpackers before anyone was even called that. No one was cheating the system. We all had valid visas and passports.

But there were the couple of bottles of whisky under the car! In a country where alcohol was banned! So lucky that that was not found. And you could definitely call that cheating the system in a Muslim country. and looking back was damn insane in a country (those countries?) like that. That felt slightly wicked occasionally but I don't think we even thought of it in relation to the Kuwait experience. But it was minor and not what we were being picked up for.

The police weren't charging us with anything, or even accusing us of anything! They could hardly do that could they.

The consul also knew someone who organises with a British guy who is working in Kuwait that Peter and I can come and share his flat. 'Some random dude' my daughter would say now, or 'a random' for short. Me first and then Peter when he is out of hospital. So there is somewhere to stay.

This guy seems quite friendly in the beginning but you know, he never says another word to us. Maybe he thought I was going to keep house and cook for him; me with my total lack of housewifely skill or interest! Or now I think, perhaps he is afraid of the hepatitis once he thinks about it, or just wants to go home to England: to normality, and we have stirred this up in him. He certainly wouldn't have been having any female company.

Like a young woman who must've been autistic who shared my house with me a few years ago, friendly when we first discussed things, so I took her on, and then never another word or smile. Disconcerting.

We were picked up because we wouldn't sleep with the Chiefs of Police! Anyway, so then began another weird time. The others are driven out to the border. The friends from all over that we had been through trauma with. I visit Peter in hospital each day and otherwise there was nowhere else for me to go. I must have suffered from claustrophobia, even then.

There was one café I could go to. It was called the Haroon Al Rasheed and there was a young guy who worked in there, and he allowed me to buy something to eat, or a cup of something. He didn't converse with me, that would have been completely forbidden, beyond me ordering something, but he must've been educated or something, or from somewhere else, like Egypt, or Iran: I think they were civilised then. Or he was just kind. Or he had a sister. He saw me as a human being.

I'm sure he was pushing the limits because here's me, still dressed in this ridiculous sleeveless, just above the knee dress that my mum made for me, white with bright flowers on, in this country where all the women are dressed in black tents outside the home.

So he is prepared to serve me and I sort of sit right over in a corner near the door so that I am barely in there. Only just in there. I know we're playing some sort of strategy that we both understand: he can let me be in the ambit of this café as long as I'm only just in there.

He keeps an eye on the door. And so do I.

I guess there is potentially big trouble for him or me or both of us, depending on who might walk in: Fundamentalist, or someone in authority, or God forbid, someone who is a combination of the two. Or using the first while in a position of the latter, for their own ends. As I have already very recently experienced there.

And he'll treat me like a person, like a normal human being instead of as a total mad alien, which I was to most people, I now see. So I can go there. So that for half an hour, I wasn't totally isolated, physically and mentally, forbidden in a forbidding place.

He was taking a big risk. It was such kindness and humanity. Dear oh dear. Still upsetting. After all this time. More than fifty years.

I was probably having one of my early bouts of PTSD (if you don't count the transmitted PTSD I feel sure I got from Daddy and from my maternal grandfather; beloved Papa: genetically, familially or culturally or all three) and I have had several new bouts since. So much so that I have to mostly write in my favourite café, which functions like a town square, because I can't stay long at home, alone.

I can't hold off the traumatic anxieties very long: especially now the flashbacks to the accumulated tragedies that have happened to me and my children, if at home too long.

They play great music in this aforementioned cafe and it has really got to me today. So great that some of the staff, the special human beings here, are sort of dancing along to it as they work.

And I am more into it this wild bluesy music than I have ever been before, in here. Somewhere down deep my poor exhausted soul is dancing too; completely for the first time ever here, although I have been coming here for years. And the music is like a dance partner to the emotional raw richness of this stuff I need to recount, even if only for a final edit.

And some of the characters who come in here too! Flamboyant and individual. I can't imagine anywhere I would rather be, including even the Far Out Far North Coast.

Writing this section in 2020, I look at the clock, I have only been writing for an hour. That doesn't feel right, it feels much longer but I suppose I have been to Kuwait and back! Across the world, across cultures and across more than half a century.

Most people would stay at home, alone for a week or two in that concrete flat. Obviously I would have had to go out to find food as well as to visit Peter, but even back then I don't think I was good at hanging at home alone. The anxiety rises. I had been diagnosed with anxiety disorder at 17.

One day I was stuck in a sandstorm in the panel van by myself. Luckily I had heard about them. I just had to sit tight as the car became totally surrounded by reddish dark. Zero vision beyond the car. Probably like being in a womb. After about fifteen minutes it gradually dispersed.

And somehow then, I get that the Lebanese man is not around for a while. Probably waiting to see if I get hepatitis too. The one with the English wife who we never meet.

When I next see him, he tells me about a job going door-to-door selling sticky fly strips that will hang from the ceiling and sell for one dinar each. One Kuwaiti Dinar equals one pound sterling back then and I can make a bit of money. Thanks anyway, but I decide I'd truly rather starve than go door-to-door selling or basically have to sell anything anywhere because of shyness. And especially here and now. It was lucky I thought that I think. I would have survived about two minutes.

Another time in Kuwait I had to run for my life to the door of the flat after I got out of the car. I had been followed by a car and then was chased to the door by a man who looked Indian! I just made it to the door and got inside and slammed it.

Was it that the whole Islamic craziness around women was contagious or something? I wondered/wonder.

I was then offered a job by a Sheikh and he's decent in that he is not after getting close to me. Says he will give me a job as a receptionist and shows me an empty office with just a typewriter. I have a quite big window near me. I don't know if he gives me, or I acquire somehow, a book on how to teach yourself to type and I start learning it. People can see he's got a blonde half-dressed, it would appear to them, receptionist in his office.

Turns out he is one of the sort of sheikhs who hires a plane to take 400 of his friends to England for the football on occasional weekends. He didn't take us: I'm sure we were slightly disappointed but it is lucky probably: very little contact with him. He never actually gives me any work to do but pays me for coming in. So we can eat.

There are stories, probably exaggerated, that the Kuwaiti people have gone straight from being nomads in the desert, with very strong rules of honour I think, to driving Cadillacs, because of the big oil finds. Westerners tell each other that when Kuwaitis get a puncture, they dump the Cadillac and buy another. Petrol is very cheap. I seem to remember one dinar per gallon. Apparently subsidised by the government.

We are all impressed by these ideas, back when there was an 'all'; when there are six of us, before Peter gets sick and the other four are deported.

And we hear that most people who live in Kuwait can't get citizenship.

We hear weddings sometimes, where the groom and friends still race up, in cars this time, not on horses, and abduct the bride and carry her off and there are sounds of triumph and gunshots into the air.

And then Peter gets out so he was only in hospital for a week or two or something like that. He's still quite sick when he gets home to this concrete place we're living in. Flattened mentally and physically.

Later Peter got work x-raying oil pipes, photography was obviously thought to be similar enough to that.

I ran into the British consul in the street about this time and he said, very keen to talk to me all of a sudden,

'I didn't know how to contact you! Questions have been asked about you in Australia, in the New South Wales Parliament and I didn't know what to tell them!'

This could probably be checked on Hansard or whatever the record is for the NSW Parliament. It is nice to think of that anchor point. Because I haven't found my old passport since the move. Since the two moves in five years. I so hope it will turn up. An iconic passport: 24 countries in 15 months and then Germany and London. I have about 15 boxes to unpack still.

I must have written to my mum which I only did occasionally. Must have written her an aerogram about my experiences in a Kuwaiti police station. She was at that stage married for a few years to a fellow, Wilfred Montgomery, who was an engineer and worked for the state government so maybe he knew how to ask questions. So that put a bit of a rocket up the up-himself consul and after that anyway he at least had our address.

Ringing overseas wasn't done then. It was very expensive. The only phone call I remember across the world, was when my mother rang me at the BBC in London another two years into our travels.

I sold my blood twice in Kuwait, not a good idea: twice within a couple of weeks it was and I fainted after the second time.

I jammed my fingers in the door going down the stairs in the Iraqi consulate after the second time and then sort of drifted/ fell down a few stairs to the bottom. I went to get visas for Iraq, the next country we needed to drive through to get to Europe. It was the only time that any of these women under black tents spoke to me. Of course they were lovely and normal under the black. We didn't share a language.

I think it was not in the Islamic tradition to give or sell blood so the hospital was happy to take it from foreigners. This group of lovely Kuwaiti women in the black tents rush over to me, like fly over to me with those tents and they point to the inside of my elbow.

I must've had a little Band-Aid in my elbow because they point at my arm and say Amiri, Amiri! Yes it was at the Amiri hospital that I had given blood again and they understood that that it made me faint and they were solicitous which was lovely.

If I was in the consulate applying for visas we must have been thinking of moving on.

I remember it being early in the day down where the truck drivers with the head scarves that I associate now with Palestinians were sculling their tiny black coffees like shots, before their long day of driving the trucks.

It was Ramadan and we were leaving Kuwait.

Greece, the Destination!

The ecstasy we felt driving down into our goal country. We stop at a taverna in a little village. We are so pleased to get there and they are so pleased that we are so pleased. We have lovely food and they give us free ouzo in little shot glasses. We know Peter is not supposed to drink after the hepatitis but we don't want to insult the villagers who are so friendly and hospitable and so we swap glasses surreptitiously and I drink his as well.

We make it to Athens!

It is the first place since Pakistan that we really want to stay for a while. It was our original reason to make the trip. So we keep an eye out for other travellers to deliver the car to England and a couple eventually take it.

We visit a friendly English bloke who is somehow living there. Out his window is the Acropolis! Right there really close and it stuns me straight away.

Present Time

I just dictated a few pages of this into a Dictaphone in a carpark in Marketown, in late summer 2021 in Newcastle, Australia where I live, and so managed to get started on Greece, which although the goal country for so long, and so deeply embedded in my heart, has been left out: for some reason, for many reasons probably!

And I will certainly find out the reasons as I write. Sigh.

I understand that in this section too, my heart is a bit wrung.

And the reason why I managed to write the first part of this big journey, up till Pakistan, was that that part was done as part of an Arts Degree. Back with not only the deadlines but especially the company, the colleagues.

To all extents and purposes I have struggled with PTSD all my life and at first some of it was inherited. And when I was 17 they didn't call it that, they called it Anxiety Disorder. And I called it I Need to Experiment with living, as well as with alcohol and recreational drugs.

I love the saying that if you are more thinking-based, life is a comedy but if you are feeling-based it is a tragedy. Well, as well as being hugely interested in the intellectual and in the more witty forms of comedy, and sometimes the more basic forms as well! my thinking always veers towards trying to save the world. The psychological truism is that that is a result of having an alcoholic (or any sort of dysfunctional perhaps) parent. Whereas my feeling for, empathy with nearly everyone and all sentient beings is almost crippling. Not good boundaries you could also call it.

It is so hard to find the right colleagues for writing. To just encourage each other and notice the journey. I sometimes teach Creative Writing and I am a Writing Mentor but I would like some more equal relationships as well.

Anyway in this section and others again I have to look at myself and sadness, not to mention tragedy. And I have to be mostly alone to write it. When I am already fighting being too much alone. On too many fronts.

Recently in my favourite café, I found again that we are always interested in the personal aren't we!

A new friend has written a memoir. He was about to pass it over to me to read the other day, in exchange for this one of mine, almost finished, when he said something interesting.

He said 'Of course I haven't put anything about any of my marriages in there!'

I found myself unconsciously turning my chair around to face him and pulling it in closer! 'Oh! How many marriages?' I said. 'Tell me!'

We all want to know what other people have been up to. And how they have survived.

That reminds me that I said to another friend recently 'Both my husbands and also the most recent important boyfriend were younger than me!'

How is that relevant to anything?

I could have said 'And I have outlived them all!' but I don't like that.

I had no idea why the Greece bit, the culmination, I thought, of that big journey should be presenting problems to write, it might be fine if I just get started. I sort of feel I've written about it but I've only mentioned it: dreamed about it, mulled on it.

I'm sitting in the car in the car park at Coles market town and it's getting warm fast so I can probably only do this for 10 minutes, I've got the engine and the air-conditioner both on actually which is very wasteful. It's been on for 10 minutes while I fluff around anyway.

I went to the beach this morning because it looked all right on the Coastal Watch Webcam thing. It looked beautiful online: sunrise and a smaller sea than I would expect after stormy weather and it was.

But when I arrived and looked at the Bar which is usually

the most sheltered place to swim I remembered it's a report for surfboard riders, not a swim report. A lot of extra sharp-looking rocks were exposed with a big rough swell on top of them, and the water was still brown from the stormy weather so you couldn't see the extent of the rocks.

So I went to Merewether Baths to have a look there. It was lovely, calmer: sunrise colours still in the sky and the water looked fantastic and I had a luscious swim. There was hardly anyone else around although it was a Saturday morning. All the other swimmers assuming, like I had really, that it probably hadn't settled down enough yet. The water was still frothy and brown from the storm, with some waves in the pool.

I got in and was entirely in there, smelling the salt water, feeling the luxury of being immersed in the fizz, looking at the entirety: sea, sky, horizon, headland, as I swam.

I didn't count laps although I was in the Baths, one of the two double Olympic sized seawater baths we have in Newcastle. The best two in the Southern Hemisphere I say, and probably the Known Universe, I always think.

I just experienced being in there like when I was a kid. I'd go for a Swim back then, not go to swim a number of laps or to count, never think about it except the desire, and if possible the actualisation, just Go for a Swim. That's why those swims and that swim was so good.

Not counting laps, or pushing myself, or worrying about whether the water was clean enough, or thinking of what I needed to do that day.

Yes seeing the Acropolis just there like that from that young guy's window in 1966 just seemed so stunningly beautiful. So right there. You could nearly touch it and it was antiquity: it was people going back thousands of years and so beautiful: so beautiful, so pretty all the white.

Yes I remember the impact of that and I remember later the friendliness of the neighbours in the flat next door to ours who showed us their baby every day: knocked on the door of our apartment and lifted up and showed their baby to us, each afternoon. I loved it. How they assumed we wanted to know.

And I loved that café's and bars everywhere were sort of mixed up and everything was based around company and food rather than primarily around alcohol like it seems to be in Australia and certainly seemed to be before I left Australia in 1965.

So yes it all looked like it was inclusive for families, looked like everyone could go including grandma and babies. And people could have food or a coffee or an alcoholic drink all together in the one place informally and the food was luscious!

All the way across including just recently through the Middle East, the food was fabulous and in Greece it was the same mix of flavour and age-old creative and slow cooking but it was just that much more relaxing to be there, the sort of civilisation I felt somehow part of.

These days I can see that a lot of what I see as a better way of life, is naïveté and what you expect of the place. I'm sure a lot of far-flung villages and islands in Greece are constrictive in their social patterning. Yuri's sister Sophia was treated badly in Athens!

Yuri, the first officer on the Patris. We met up with his sister. He had given us her contact details and we went out to the Plaka with her. We have a photo and she's in it at a café with us there. But I got the impression that she was really looked down upon by the couple of men we were also with. I didn't know why.

Was it because she was a bit liberated? Perhaps she had been married and left a husband I don't know but there was this not good feeling about how they were thinking of her. Did they say she was like a prostitute? So I'm sure it is not all blissful.

We also met a Socrates there! An ordinary youngish Greek guy.

But I loved Greece. I loved Athens.

I love Syntagma: Constitution square: the feeling of neighbourhood people getting together around simple café tables or in squares. It felt like that was the way the city had grown. It encouraged getting together, rather than encouraging people to go off into the suburbs and their own house or flat, like the apartness of suburban life that I'd left behind in Sydney.

Syntagma was still fantastic when I went back there in 2013. By then I appreciated the political and philosophical depth as well.

So that's why I've kept off Greece? Because it was my heart's desire?

We went to Mykonos, It was the only island we went to back then, and it was all white buildings and very touristy. It has been deliberately kept that all the buildings had to match and be picture postcard perfect. It had a few boutique type shops, and we went to a dress designer and I tried on a couple of shimmering things and the fellow got me to stay there for a couple of hours modelling because some of the older women off ships took notice of the clothes on me. I asked Peter to go back to our room and get the camera you know about 10 minutes walk at the most and come back and take a picture but he didn't want to.

And maybe I feel funny about Greece because I don't know, he had some sort of very short meeting with some young waitress. The woman on Mykonos who I thought was a bit prostituting, had her eye on him. I don't know but when I said well what was that about, when he appeared a very short time later he refused to tell me and I didn't have the sort of sense of security and of myself to be able to handle that very well. I mean it was just internalised but it mattered.

In fact, I obviously haven't got over it yet! LOL. Fifty-five years later when I am writing this Kuwait to London section because I realised it should be in.

It's not that I didn't have my own admirers. There was a black American who was a great dancer who told me he would come and fetch me anywhere in the world if I just said the word. He was very attractive but I didn't believe him and I was committed.

That was when I was working for this rather awful man in a bar in Piraeus as a waitress. It was a bar for American servicemen of some sort so maybe this was getting close to the sort of post-war Allied forces that we were to end up working for in Germany. The next country.

But you know that things hit me so stupidly hard like Peter disappearing briefly with some girl. Anything to do with not being wanted.

I remember that wonderful story of that female traveller but I still haven't learnt that moral. I think it's in a Virago Press of Women Travellers book. A woman telling her story, in The States, back in the first part of the 20th Century. Her man does her wrong, shows a lack of interest and so she thinks 'Oh Well' and hops a freight train to another place. And I mean hops. How poor people back then when a train slowed down, would bravely jump on and hold tight... It was the Oh Well, Other Pastures that grabbed me.

I have been able to do that about locations, occupations, but I have always wanted love to last.

But yes, another silly little thing which really tripped me up and still does was that the man who owned that café had a St Christopher medal and he said he was all right driving around the dangerous roads nearby because he had the medal and people who didn't have one weren't Catholic and they might get killed on the road with the inference that it wouldn't matter. But then that would be the full sort of, you know that total depth of superstitious type religious thinking. But why would I not just accept it and laugh it off. I would you know argue with myself exclaim to myself about it for the next, for the next forever 50 years almost.

I suppose it is just part of my lifelong obsession with Ethics and Philosophy that culminated in my studying for an Arts Degree with a double major in Philosophy and English and a minor in Linguistics in my forties.

So yes I have a strange sense of ethics and morality and probably too much of the latter for my own good.

We gambled with Yuri's friends. I can only remember one afternoon of it. That was enough. It was probably only an hour or two. I mean we wouldn't have had much money we were only ever a few days ahead at the best but we played Dealers Choice Poker. You can tell what that is, it's in the title isn't it.

We would have only played a few games of poker in our lives.

You could tell that these guys had played plenty of poker by the attentive way they sat.

So Dealers Choice is when the person shuffling the cards turns to deal, only then they announce we are playing this sort of poker. 'These are the rules.' So very fast gambling with the rules changing with every hand, with every dealer. I think it took us about an hour to lose all our money.

How stupid! I can laugh now. I think it was not good at the time.

I remember apart from the Acropolis only a few fabulous antiquities including at Corinth which I just loved. I took a photo there of a little girl skip skipping through one of the main ruins. By then I'd learned a thing or two about photography from Peter. The two things show each other: the tiny little new person amidst that very old beautiful stone antiquity.

I can't bring myself to look at photos and I'll need to bring myself to look at photos alone probably, for this. It's funny. It's as if I can now be only a few hours by myself a day to try and get some writing done, and I don't want to do anything else by myself. Let alone photos with their embedded feelings of loss.

Except I will watch Vera on tv once a week on Saturday afternoon. And I would do the same for Endeavour if it was on at the moment. But even Vera feels a bit borderline whether I should be watching it, because sometimes they are very grim, very sad.

The fact that they are set in England, and Endeavour especially in London about the time when we were there, when I was young (and happy) is an element too.

Germany

We actually hitch-hiked from Greece to Germany, having sent the car on to its owners' parents in England via some more travellers.

We journeyed day and night through Europe in a truck. I remember we went through a checkpoint in Yugoslavia where the border guards had to have a photo taken with me, the blond hair I suppose. I have that photo somewhere.

There was also a stop in an all-night little Italian coffee place. So we had a corner of Yugoslavia and a corner of Italy. The truck was stopping in Munich so that's where we got off.

We somehow met a young English bilingual guy Rod who was living in Munich and he let us stay on the floor in his room for the first couple of nights.

He took us to watch the World Cup Soccer Final up on a TV in a bar in town. It was being played in London. It must've been July 30th 1966. It was mostly young Germans in there, with a sprinkling of English-speaking travellers or expatriates.

They were so welcoming in that bar. If our team scored, they bought us beer with schnapps chasers, and when Germany scored we English speakers bought the drinks.

It was my first experience of soccer and so exciting and happy. It was played out to a penalty decider and England won! The young Germans certainly remained totally friendly and hospitable to the end.

Perhaps back then, soccer was, in Germany anyway, an interest of the younger, more internationally thinking progressive citizens. A game that crossed borders. Or we just chanced on a good bar!

I had certainly never watched a game of soccer before, perhaps not even heard of it.

We found work in the Kaserne: McGraw Kaserne, by then an American Army base. 'Oh Shame oh Bloody Horror!' I was to say with a wry smile in later anti-war activist years. 'We worked for the American Army!' Still they weren't waging war there but part of an occupying force. And it stopped us from starving. Humanity's usual bottom line excuse.

It was pretty awful for me working there: at first in the supermarket on a checkout. I never learnt to differentiate quickly enough, the values of the American green dollar notes that looked all the same to me, and so I gave the wrong change.

So then they put me in the mechanical supplies place which I remember as being a windowless under-ground sort of a place, maybe a former bunker I finally realise.

It was better for Peter whom they employed as a photographer and gave the use of a big Polaroid camera even after-hours, which made him a hit socially. I have a few of those pictures. He used to say that his work seemed to be mainly photographing crashed helicopters.

We were given rooms in sex-segregated big concrete blocks. I had probably not even heard the word gender back then.

We ate every night in the local family-owned restaurant/bar. As well as great family food, it of course served plenty of beer. It was such fun because we made friends with young travellers from all over the world. Every night there was good German food and also warmth as the weather started to cool, with lots of friendly conversation and debate.

I suppose that those of us travelling on the cheap and working everywhere at that time tended to have a great sense of curiosity, a very good sign in a person I think. Back in that day and age. Long before travel became a commodity.

I was particularly interested in two very intelligent young Jewish guys from Brooklyn with their soft accents and their ideas. One of them, Marty, and I became quite close. He wanted to get to Israel and help them protect their land and identity. The other guy, who taught us to play Bridge, was also interested in seeing Israel but totally against 'nationalism' including Israel's which he said always leads to war. Very prescient of him. I have written more about those evenings in the article on Booze.

The Kaserne was all English-speaking but I took German lessons to add to my one year of German in second-year high school where it had felt like the only foreign language that I might be able to pronounce properly. I had been streamed into the highest science and maths plus languages.

I was interested in getting work where I would learn the language faster. I told the lovely young German woman teaching the weekly German language evening class I attended, and she offered to help me see what work was available.

She took me to have a look at a small lens making factory. We went into this room of silent older women, probably in their 40s and 50s. They just stared at me as I was introduced. I got an inkling of the underlying distrust and probably hatred from the older generation. Just as back home in Australia it still existed for German and Japanese people I must admit. (And those nationals didn't happen to be back-packing around Aus in those days!)

We were like an anachronism, from the future.

My family had always been concerned about social justice for everyone, especially people who were the worst-off but they were certainly prejudiced about anyone on the other side in WW2, or who might have been.

Much later on in 2021, I am so aware of the ramifications of the Second World War, even now. How much more back then?

Perhaps the after-shock waves were so intense back then, even for thinking people, that not many objective views were available.

I was to feel a bit more of the undercurrent once when I got on a bus in Munich. Because I had blonde hair and blue eyes people always assumed that I was German and expected me to know things that I didn't. By then I had learnt to say 'Ich spreche kein Deutsch, aber ich verstehe eine kleine'. 'I don't speak German but I understand a little'. The 2nd phrase was supposed to stop anyone being nasty behind my back I think!

The young German conductress didn't believe that I didn't understand her in some argument about the fare or where I wanted to go or something so she made me get off the bus!

I went back to where Rod, our first friend in Germany lived, and told him about it, feeling quite upset. He marched me into town, into the transport office and with his wonderful bilingual skills, demanded an apology for me. Which we got.

I read *The Rise and Fall of the Third Reich* by William L. Shirer but I refused to read *Mein Kampf* which was written by Hitler himself.

I started to get the feeling that all of us English-speaking travellers but especially Marty and the other young Jewish guy might actually not be safe there.

Looking it up now, I see that *The Rise and Fall* is 1245 pages!

In my memory I have always thought that I read it all but I wonder now whether I had the time and staying power for such a tome. I have always been hungry for knowledge and it was in Germany that I noticed that my total lack of understanding of modern history, except as funnelled through my pacifist grandfather, was a serious defect.

It was only in my 60s that my half-sister told me that our maiden name, Goodman, is Jewish. We are all a melting pot and had better not forget it.

It was after all, only 20 years since the Second World War! No wonder my mum sounded anxious about me being there. I'd only just started to understand it in a visceral way. As those involved in the fighting, or living under it must certainly have felt it. I don't even know if Munich was bombed. I will look it up.

It is still interesting now to think back to that probably very big division between some progressive young people, who we just happened to meet in a bar the day after we arrived in Munich, but who represented a big groundswell of those who grew up after the war, who wanted to be friends and wanted totally to disassociate with what their parents' generation had done in the war. As we travellers did too. And others, particularly older Germans who had lived through that war.

Issues that I was at least partially awake to as well. Having taken on my poor family about Hiroshima when I found out about it at age 12. I had seen that we weren't entirely the 'goodies' as represented in all the great war movies then playing on the new TV. An awful understanding for me and hard on the family.

It was in Munich that I really started to think about what had happened to the Jews.

I was to meet another terrific representative of the new German revolutionary youth in a few months in London.

Much later I was interested to see just how far progressive German thinking went even into getting the wrong end of the stick, when some students attacked the Australian Philosopher Peter Singer who was supposed to be giving a lecture there.

I have studied Singer as part of a Philosophy Major here at Newcastle University in Australia and so know his work a bit. His ideas are what I think of as progressive ie for the good of the whole species and biosphere going forward.

They include him wanting to liberalise the law around mercy killing when babies are born with very serious problems. He wants the parents in discussion with the doctors, to be aided in making decisions about whether their children should be helped to survive or not. Rather than have to battle against the assumptions of keeping a baby alive at any costs. If she or he is to have no quality of life.

Like the baby born without most of its brain whom I had nursed in North Ryde Psychiatric Hospital when I was 17.

I assume that it was this argument that brought Singer down in Germany. The progressive Germans were unfortunately reminded of Hitler's eugenics, or the killing off of all sections of society that he saw as less than perfect.

They couldn't tolerate to listen to Singer because he reminded them of the possible dark sides of that argument if it was taken too far. They ordered him off the stage and when he dropped his glasses in the jostle, someone trod on them. People were shouting 'Singer Aus! Meaning Singer Get Out' which reminded him of how his Jewish antecedents were treated in Germany in the war.

It is ironic because my reading of Singer on this subject is that he is strongly motivated by compassion and a desire to help the suffering of new parents in that situation. As well as great on logic of course, as everyone who goes anywhere in Philosophy has to be.

Photo 3 Restaurant/Bar, Munich 1966

In Munich, I am 2nd from the left. Paul Delofski is 4th from the left. In that great local café/bar. Photo Peter Bellmaine.

Vilification Unhelpful in Lockout Debate

(Printed in The Newcastle Herald on the 5th May 2021)
by Newcastle Writer and Health Worker, Paula Morrow.

In the Lockout Laws debate, some people claim that everything that is wrong with present-day economics and social organisation is the fault of the generation born immediately after WW2, now combined with the civic-minded people who are presently trying to wind back the abuse of alcohol and the death and destruction that this abuse causes.

So some people's idea of a great city is one which has many places where you can drink all night?

When I was a young back-packer working in Munich, Germany, we often wanted to talk or rock on after the local restaurant/alcohol place shut at midnight but the only choice was back to one of our rooms or very small flats.

We felt like we could go on carousing for hours but usually after walking there, sometimes through deep, slushy snow and consuming only half a drink more, the most urgent impulse was to go to sleep on the couch or if necessary, the carpeted floor.

This kept us safe.

That drinking threshold that tips us over into sleep, I think can also push us over into mad or violent behaviour if people are upright in crowded streets or venues.

It wouldn't matter so much if we were a culture that put company and the sharing of food first and where the alcohol (usually but not necessarily, wine) is an add-on.

Our society however, is one where we chuck the alcohol

down before we eat or often, even before we meet. It has been hugely dangerous on the road always, and has only improved with the driving/drinking laws and of course they can't be policed adequately.

So we know alcohol with driving is dangerous and now we are coming to know that drunkenness is a big issue in other areas: on our streets and in our homes.

The understanding we now have of (usually) young people being killed or brain-damaged by a vicious drunken punch is now augmented by facing our serious rates of domestic violence, very often fuelled by alcohol.

As for the argument that the immediate post World War Two generation has somehow ruined it for this generation.

I would take a much longer viewpoint and say that un-controlled capitalism is well on the way to ruining the planet for all of us, particularly now, where everything has hotted up and there are machines that can knock down a whole forest in days.

We all need to join with groups that are working for the goals of a cohesive, sustainable community, not start inciting inter-generational strife, or vilification of any section of our society.

Germany is way ahead of Australia in the fight to prevent more climate damage and save a liveable atmosphere for the world's children. They have a more representative democracy which led to The Greens being much more represented in parliament since the early 1980s.

They have set the world standards for passive house design so that buildings need the minimum of energy to maintain a liveable temperature.

And Germany with its long freezing cold winters is far ahead of us in the use of solar energy!

When Fukushima went off, Angela Merkel was the only world leader who gave me some hope for the future. Merkel, who has a PhD in Physical Chemistry, came out within a day or two and said 'The unthinkable has become the thinkable with Fukushima. Germany is going to close down all its nuclear reactors and we are going to start the shut-down of the oldest one today'.

Flashback to some of my earliest influences

My Mum Olga Goodman (nee Purkis), had joined the WAAF aged about 18 in 1941. She didn't leave Australia but she told me that she had flown sitting in the bottom of a bomber. It would have been a liberating time for her. There are several photos of her having a laugh with a lot of young Australian soldiers.

Some of whom did not come home.

She later got together with my father who had seen too much action and became a bit of a cot-case from it. They got married, had me straight after the war, in January 1946. He finished a law degree in double quick time and they went to Tasmania where he taught Jurisprudence: The Philosophy and Theory of Law.

I remember her looking pretty on a tennis court in a little white skirt and top. She told daddy's sister Dinah that it was really a man's world down in Tassie.

He started drinking disastrously, I don't know how often. We would call it PTSD now and he would get help for it. He was tender and loving to me.

I remember him coming home and being helped inside by a mate and vomiting into a metal bucket that mum handed the mate. I was concerned for him and rushed forward to help. But mum held me back indicating disapproval 'No! he's been bad!' I felt fear and confusion.

I remember my daddy talking on the radio. I would have been three. Much later I asked Mum about that. At first she had forgotten and then she said, 'Oh! Yes! He was calling the Rugby!' He had played Rugby Union for Gordon (Auntie Dinah told me that the University team had wanted him as well). He was a fast *runner and a sportsman as well as brilliant.*

I remember saying to mum about that time 'Peter Peter Pumpkin Eater, had a wife and couldn't keep her, that's true isn't it mummy?'

Not long after, she took me and left him and we went to live with her parents and brother in my grandparents' rented flat in Manly.

Our plane was forced down in a field on that trip. Must have been fog or mechanical problems. Some farmers' wives brought porridge out for us!

I vomited with severe motion sickness in any plane or car trip as a child but I remember that, unlike other passengers, I wasn't afraid of this unconventional landing. I think that Mum remained very interested in aeroplanes and found the incident a bit exciting and I felt that from her!

My Dad, Peter Goodman, had joined up just as an enlisted man, not applied to be an officer, but been taken into Duntroon for a quickie 3 months officers' course after winning a half mile and then a one mile running race straight afterwards at some army do. He was in Europe and Nth Africa, but then PNG including Kokoda where he got malaria and dysentery and lost a third of his body weight while fighting against the Japanese in the jungle. He credited having walked out, one of only two in his group who managed to do that, rather than be carried, with helping in his survival.

He came back and did a law degree in 18 months short of the normal time. He was in the same bright year as Lionel Murphy and Neville Wran; he beat the lot and won the university medal. But he was soon to become more and more alcoholic, one of those swift declines. No help for him or my mum back then.

London

It was fortuitous that when I went to the hairdresser last Thursday (2020) for the first time in at least six months, because of Covid 19, I had a young woman called Bella do my hair. She turned out to have a sister who is married to an Englishman and they live in London. Bella has been there a few times and it was great to talk to her: to re-live living in England a bit.

I certainly loved London and loved working for the BBC. I think Peter and I relied on each other again more and the relationship was very happy again. Peter was working as a fashion photographer and fashion was always his main interest, although talent dripped around him every time he picked up a camera. Or went into a darkroom.

I think that Germany had been a bit of a strain on us, with the heavy drinking until late every night, where we had lots of kindred souls and we had to sleep in separate blocks, the female ones of which were incredibly bleak concrete inside as well as out. Mine had a mattress on the floor and an immersion jug that you could boil water in that I had acquired and that was about it.

For some reason the male ones were a bit more furnished, at least where Peter was, not that I was supposed to see inside his room.

Certainly if I ever think I should have stopped anywhere in my life it was in London working for the BBC. (And for *Stuff* a couple of years later in North Sydney!) Not that it was directly intellectually fulfilling but I was appreciated and it was at one remove intellectual. I was working for The Listener and you can't get more cerebral than that! Probably I wasn't reading more than a little of the magazine which was incredibly arcane but a few of us formed a little film group and on Mondays after work we would go and take a big reel off the shelves and watch a film. There were a huge number of choices.

When we first arrived in London people came looking for tenants where we landed, and we went to stay with this man and his wife also called Paula and their children in Turnham Green and it was all right for a while, but she was very tumultuous: moody and shouted at her family and one day I shouted back from upstairs and that was the end of that. I don't think that they told us we had to move but I think that we felt that we had better.

I first worked at Heathrow Airport as a filing clerk, but then got a job in Hammersmith, working in a travel agency as an accounts clerk. I was alone upstairs with this poor older woman who'd lost a husband to cancer and she gave me blow by blow descriptions of that heart-rending process. Easily made despondent, I left there.

Luckily I got a job with the BBC at The Listener in Marylebone High Street. I would take my banana sandwich brought from home, upstairs on to the roof by myself at lunchtime and look out over London, including the dome of St Paul's Cathedral. There were always a couple of gigantic cranes about in the middle distance, but it was quiet up there and I loved London: I was in love with London.

Peter and I saw a flyer for the film, *The Seventh Seal* put up somewhere and went to see it. It was being shown in someone's big house or office one night. The group of people hosting it were called *The Process* and were all dressed in white and had solemn expressions and Alsatian dogs. They seemed slightly weird but that didn't matter.

And then the impact of that Ingmar Bergman movie! Probably the most dramatic and the most philosophical that I have ever seen. That little family, travelling across plague-torn Europe, playing chess with Death and so greatly out-matched…it seared through to my soul.

Weekend directed by Godard, is the other stupendous movie I remember seeing in London.

The English pub situation seemed ideal, civilised. Certainly compared to Germany or compared to Australia! They were open around lunchtime, closed for a few hours and then open around dinner time for a few hours again.

I studied modern history at night: Europe in WW2, and Economics, and got my O levels for both. The lecturer, who must have been a leftie, said that there is no better product than a bomb, for a capitalist. You just throw them away and buy new ones!

It reminds me of the Quaker idea of addictive products, perhaps even heroin, being the 'best' product for a capitalist to promote. But this was much later at Quaker Yearly Meeting in about 1989 in Sydney. Burnum Burnum the aboriginal activist was there too and was such a clever and wise man. He had gone over and declared possession of England for Aboriginal people in 1988! He and our youngest, little Abigail aged five, got on very well!

I had been streamed towards Maths and Science and Languages at Narrabeen Girls' High, a great school academically. But it meant I only did 6 months of history and that was in First Year. It was wonderful Ancient History: Egypt, with the red-haired woman teacher whom I was a bit afraid of, Mrs Thompson I think her name was.

In England I had some vague idea of applying to Oxford, the

only university that I had heard of, perhaps. And in London started doing A levels at night towards that.

It was only decades later that I found out that my father had wanted to go to Oxford too, had applied for a Rhodes Scholarship to that end. His sister, Dinah said that his application was considered invalid because he had finished his law degree in 18 months short of the usual time!

I'll have to check that out with my sister Linda. She has a very different view of our father, Peter Goodman, to that held by his sister Dinah because Linda and her younger sister Susie suffered badly from his alcoholism. I suffered from it too but in a different way: from being taken away from him when my mother took me and left him. I experienced it as a hidden gulf, a pervading sadness, because he had been gentle and loving with me. Whereas Linda and Susie lived for years with him totally demoralised in a singlet, as their mum stuck it out for a long time.

It was exacerbated for me I think, because he was never allowed to be spoken about again - such a pity that. Apparently after he visited in Manly when I was four or five, I ran after him down the street, yelling 'I want my daddy!' so you can see why my mother and grandfather may have decided to make such a decision.

And such a pity that he did not find and commit to Alcoholics Anonymous. Instead of, his second family told me much later, having endless therapy? conversations with a charismatic female Dr Stella Dalton at Wisteria House. He probably engaged with her intellectually, and she with him. Always the possibility for great distraction there.

We made friends with Julie and Richard Ivey from South Australia when we four arrived in the UK at the same time. They were making silver jewellery (with gas cylinder soldering equipment!) at home on the carpeted floor in the lounge room of their rented old house, in Bethnal Green.

They ended up teaching us some of those skills. Peter was good at it. I never overcame my fear of the gas bottle. Peter did a bit more of it when we were back in Australia. I still have some of those pieces and wear them. I made moccasins and sold them at Paddy's Market. We were renting a house in Clareville where there were still koalas in the trees.

Richard particularly liked to go to the movies on Monday mornings. Films we called them then I think, even perhaps still, as in my childhood and youth, 'the pictures'. He particularly needed to break down stereotypical ways of living and thought it was great to be at the pictures at that time of the week, instead of in a suit somewhere in an office.

I liked the idea of that but I was happy to be at the BBC on Monday mornings.

We next lived in a comfortable large bed-sitting room in a lovely old shared house in Chiswick with our own kitchenette and a shared bathroom which was often the go. It was owned and run very well by an older man.

I applied at the BBC for a film camera cadetship they called them back then and I got an interview but the man said very kindly 'But dear we don't employ women! You'd have to go into war zones!' and I thought well do I want to go to war zones? I hadn't thought that through but he offered me an editing cadetship instead which was a rather exciting prospect.

I found nothing but appreciation at the BBC, including from my two bosses: Mr Thurston and Miss Leat. Except from the young woman I shared an office with who turned a bit nasty when she decided I must be a communist because I thought garbage men should be paid more and medical specialists less, because the latter got more work satisfaction! And status I would say now.

Welsh Bill, and Libby, Australian, who were friends from our time in Munich and some of the others from that period, were over in London too and we got together with them for Christmas. It snowed! This was apparently rare for Christmas in London and so lovely.

I suddenly thought 'Why do we all drink so much?' and stopped that Christmas binge-out. Just as well, it was to transpire.

Mum sent me a bit of money for my 21st at the end of January, 1967, to go out for dinner. We went to a restaurant by the Thames. I had sole, and a glass of something, that was my idea of pleasure and sophistication then. Still is. I have put a meal like that in Life In Time, my first novel. I remember at that quiet birthday dinner thinking that I wouldn't mind a coffee or a second glass of something, and to sit here longer, but we had used up mum's birthday money and so we went home.

Paris January 1968

Peter and I went to Paris for a week and stayed in a very cheap little place off the Place Saint Michel. It was a 22nd birthday celebration for me and we had saved ahead for it.

The travellers now internalised in us knew to notice the workers' cafes and to eat in them. No-one spoke English in them but we were accepted and given wonderful-tasting meat and vegetable casserole meals with carafes of wine for hardly any cost.

I loved Paris. We weren't far from the Seine where artists painted, we walked a lot and travelled a bit on the Metro. We had the tiniest balcony off our room and were provided croissants for breakfast.

I tried to speak French when buying from a man in a kiosk by the Seine but he just frowned at me and I never tried again. I might have done 5 years of French in High School but only 5 marks were for 'oral', the rest was for the written language. Australia was a very long way from Europe in those days.

We came upon an enormous protest march in our week in Paris! Or rather it came upon us! We were caught by it, with a few others in a narrow Parisian street. All these thousands of people led by about eight mature men in greatcoats, perhaps unionists, arms linked, severe expressions, all shouting 'Johnson! Assassin!' Referring to the American President, Lyndon Johnson and the continuation of the Vietnam War.

The two words sounded so good together, with the alliteration of Johnson with the French pronunciation of Assassin! March, march, march march, 'John son! As sass an!'

We had to press ourselves into a doorway and wait till the thousands had passed! It took ages. An amazing show of people power and caring.

I remember going up the concrete stairs at The Louvre because we wanted to see the Mona Lisa. That was unusually touristy for us actually. It felt like there was something wrong with my knees! I had to drag my legs up the stairs; they had no power.

Back in London

I didn't say anything to Peter but soon after, back in London waiting for the bus to go to work at the BBC I fainted at the bus stop. I could see Peter on the other side of the road going to his work but he didn't see me and I couldn't call out.

I can't remember who rescued me at the bus stop but as soon as I could, I took myself to the doctor and found out I was pregnant which was a big shock with only a slight very recent suspicion of something wrong: with the knees in the Louvre, and the fainting episode.

Now that I was pregnant the landlord at the good Chiswick place said we had to leave before the baby was born, even though we were only going to be there for a couple of months with the bub before we came home to Australia. We had decided to go home pretty well straight after I became pregnant. It had sort of decided itself. They had a strict no babies or children rule in that house. Afraid of crying potentially affecting other tenants I suppose.

That was good because we got a flat with Mrs Early who was an Australian expatriate, a lovely woman who happily took us in, even though it was only for a couple of months.

'No problem!' she said with a smile.

It was south of the river at The Oval and Mrs Early had a garden where she happily worked. She often pointed out a beautiful bloom as we came and went to work. What a lovely woman! The archetypal beautiful landlady.

She had room for my mother soon too, when she visited from Australia. She gave Mum a small bedroom with its own toilet and wash basin next door, near our flat. It must have been a big old house.

In London I felt that I belonged, especially after the rest of the journey I suppose! And that there was untold possibility. At first there was the recognition that a lot of people notice: the street and station names from Monopoly. A lot of my ancestry was English, with a bit of Swedish/Finnish/Russian thrown in, but I have never played Northern European Monopoly.

Much that I have been influenced by my love for Greece and much that I am interested in Aboriginal culture, I did not grow up knowing anything about them.

Intellectual and aesthetic possibility I suppose I felt in London. And in Paris. And Athens.

In Newcastle Australia, I am feeling the opposite which is not very good! Well the world is having a hard time now with this pandemic and many other things.

I just hope that young people are feeling something hopeful, exciting, the potentiality of the world and their lives. Certainly sometimes in the environmental protest movement, I think you can find it. In the camaraderie.

I am sure I would have found the intellectual buzz in Berlin too. And many other places. I may still make it there. I only fly if I feel it is essential, because of concern about emissions now. It needs to be like a pilgrimage for my work almost, or for my individuation: the Jungian term which to me means deep psychological integration.

On that huge 3-year, 26 country journey of discovery, we only had three short half-hour hops in airplanes. Between Kathmandu and India, and between London and Paris and return. The rest was overland or by boat.

And I have flown twice in the last seven years as well. Long haul to Greece in 2013 and to Vietnam in 2018.

If I go again I will try for boat and train.

We were monolingual and monocultural in 50s and early 60s Australia. We were absorbing immigrants: I had school friends from Holland, Italy and Egypt. They and aboriginal people were however expected to drop their former affiliations and become Anglo Saxon.

It is so much better since we have become multicultural although I must admit to a wariness of Islam, especially I find it upsetting if I see a woman with her face covered. It reminds me of the experiences in Kuwait and feels like the Middle Ages to me, or do I mean the Dark Ages.

In London we were confronted by police horses in a small early demo against the Vietnam War, in what seemed like a fenced off park in the middle of London. It may have been the American Embassy in Grosvenor Square and it was pivotal for me. I was about 6 months pregnant. I was in my little black and white thinly striped dress that was luckily the shape to encompass pregnancy.

There was a line of police on beautiful white horses. For some reason Peter and I were down at the front. Perhaps we were up the back and they came in behind us and we all turned around? All of a sudden the line of police horses and riders facing us, already too tall, were made to rear up in some sort of show of strength and power. It was very scary. I was conscious of my unborn baby.

I think it was the first protest I actually took part in.

My mother rang me from Australia. She rang the BBC and asked for me and was terribly impressed that they put her straight through, when they had hundreds of thousands of employees throughout the country.

Photo 4 Anti-Vietnam-War Protest, London 1968

Photo David Hurn Anti-Vietnam War Rally Grosvenor Square London May 1968.

And the first thing she said after 'Is that you Paula?' was 'You sound like a bloody pom!' And announced that she was coming over.

This sounds slightly humorous now, as I remember a common saying of my mum's, back in Aus, was 'whinging pom'. I don't know if there was something in the English accent of the migrating peoples (that included us only a couple of generations before) that reverberated as a whine against the Australian drawl, or whether she thought people were not appreciative enough of their new land.

I don't know who Peter was doing his fashion photography with in London, but I remember that he said that Helmut Newton told him that he Peter, was second only to himself, in talent over there! And Peter was only 21 by then.

Gisela was this lovely German fashion model that Peter was to take photographs of. I remember thinking, I won't be able to compete here, and we're going out to dinner afterwards with her and her husband as well!

But the husband turned out to be a young German revolutionary involved in all the fabulous uprisings happening in Germany and Europe! He and I just talked on excitedly about the state of the world and the revolution for hours during the photo shoot. And we couldn't stop after it, over dinner, while Peter and Gisela just sat around.

I wonder whether those ethereal photos Peter took of Gisela have survived anywhere. I doubt it.

His second wife Merle, who was lovely, and kind to me, was a born-again person. Photography may not have been on her list of worthwhile or even allowable, things.

Zelma of the dry wit, mother of Julie and Peter, was my first mother-in-law. Merle told her early in their relationship, 'I'm a Christian'.

Zelma replied, 'Aren't we all?'

I think that that was very good. I don't even know if Zel was being funny. It was how our insular Australian society felt.

I can't blame life or Merle that Peter didn't keep up his photography and he didn't seem to want to when he got back to Australia. Mind you I wouldn't have seemed to have wanted to be keeping up with doing any writing either. We were probably affected by so many things we had not foreseen: not just new parenthood and moving back across the world. I am only really seeing that now, years after both Peter and my second husband have died.

Going Home

We came back on the maiden voyage of the Russian boat, the Shota Rustaveli. It was four weeks with a nine-week-old baby and just one stop for re-fuelling, and then Fremantle and then Sydney. Luckily I love ships.

The life on board the ship included demonstrations of amazing Georgian Cossack dancing by some of the crew.

A humorous cultural difference showed up between the Russian crew and the mostly Australian passengers. Because it was the maiden voyage, there were a few free bottles of wine on every table every night.

I was luckily pretty careful not to drink too much with a little breast-fed baby, asleep on the floor in his basket near our table, but most people were not so inhibited. The Russian officers drank solidly and stolidly behind the captain's table and gradually sank way down in their seats until they seemed almost comatose. Whereas the Australians, including us sometimes, ended up in conga lines loudly dancing, bopping and stamping around the ship!

I was washing nappies in the boiler room, helping with the talks in the library about the Vietnam War and Conscription issues, organised by Brian Laver and his wife Janita and having a couple of games of bridge, as well as surviving the voyage with a very young baby. One night for some reason, there must have been something special on, we left baby Carlos with a stewardess to babysit in the cabin. When we came back he was swaddled from head to foot. He looked like a baby Egyptian mummy and he looked surprised. It didn't feel right and we didn't do that again.

It reminds me of the first time ever I met a Russian person, a journalist, in the Middle East. I fully expected philosophy-speaking, glass-throwing over the shoulder mad intellectualism. From reading Dostoevsky, especially The Brothers Karamazov at 17. Thanks to my Mum doing a 6 week night course on European Literature through the WEA, and BUYING the books. They were around the unit when I got out of B Hall and had a bit of spare time.

But the Russian journalist was so disappointing, so pedestrian. As we all would be when compared to those dazzlingly intellectually alive characters in that book. Weird our expectations.

When the boat was nearly in Fremantle after our four-week one stop voyage, the first radio contact I heard, the first direct link with Australia, was the old advertising jingle, 'Take Vincents! With Confidence! For Quick Three-Way Relief!' The same old jingle. The worst sort of mind-altering! It was as if we had gone back in time.

We stopped at Fremantle and had a couple of hours shore leave. I gave baby Carlos some tinned milk out of a bottle, not wanting to breast-feed in public. Soon after we got back to the ship and Peter lay down in the cabin for a nap, the baby started projectile vomiting.

I ran with the bub and found the British fellow who was the intermediary between us and the crew. He started running with me to find the ship's doctor, who like all the crew except the librarian, spoke no English. But I showed him the tin that had held the milk and he threw it out of the porthole in disgust which certainly made his point.

He then led us down to the kitchens and instructed one of the chefs to supply us with weak black tea for the baby which we were to alternate with the water off cooking the rice in the huge pots, for the next few hours. And yes, no more vomiting. A scary time.

I think now, that the loss of 'Swinging London', with Europe nearby, unconsciously hit both of us hard. Australia was so parochial back then.

It was like going from the centre of things to the periphery.

We faced Australia again: including for me the death of both my grandparents while I was away.

Now, with grandchildren myself, I don't know how I could have gone off for three years and left those grandparents who had been more like parents to me.

But too, I do remember the wonder of sailing into stunningly beautiful Sydney Harbour on a glistening golden and blue October day in 1968.

Photo 5 The Shota Rustaveli 1968

A 28 day voyage with one stop to refuel.

Goodbye to Paula and Peter a poem by Paul Delofski

Bursting into chill, dry air;

perspiration boiling out

through my thin shirt;

- Gasping from frantic

running past broken

English of Greek

stewards and blur of

unreal cabin numbers

in the huge hum and throb

of lower decks – looking for you;

the ship's sad horn

prodded me down the gangplank.

The echo of the purser's voice

and disappointment mocked

my panic with each step;

until, turning to seal my

failure with a final sweep

I saw you.

You stood away,

arms linked, alone

against the black night,

some bright light coldly

catching your faces

and carving you (for

what may be forever.

See you in London I called,

turned not looking behind me

and ran pounding out into

the pale yellow lane.

Perhaps,

the new girl beside me

could have half-understood

the flashing of tears

that eased the acid throat

and choke of my anguish.

Perhaps…

The Patris was the ship that took us away from Australia. It's funny, two years later we were living in a crumbling old building in Kirribilli where the harbour lapped against the stone of the lower storey. One night I suddenly felt electrified more than usual by the life going past on the water and looked out to see an iridescent ship, and it was our Patris again, except it didn't feel like it was 'us' anymore, and it's hard to celebrate when you're feeling estranged.

I still wonder. I like a lot of solitude. I still wonder, how do you celebrate alone?

A Note

A young woman brought a note home from pre-school when her child started there, suggesting that parents may like to consult with their elders re food to send along with the kids. She showed this to her friend, also a new mum and it was met with amazed mirth! Elders? They decided that the flyer must have been meant for parents of the few indigenous children at the pre-school.

As the mother of one of these young women, and a nutritionist as well, this gave me pause.

.But it takes a lot of time and energy to re-invent the wheel and meanwhile we are wasting the planet.

If we live in a society that doesn't value its elders and wisdom generally, only the latest adolescent looks and celebrities, then the young won't have anything to look forward to in their middle to old age.

I wouldn't have been so deeply shocked to find myself with young children sheltering in the bathroom of a twisting, tearing house, if it had been general knowledge that there had been an earthquake in Newcastle 60 years ago.

My beautiful grandfather who was a stretcher-bearer in the fields of France in the First World War told me when I was 12, about the absolute folly and disgrace of governments who send young men to kill each other and die in useless wars. Must we discover everything over and over again.

Fun in the Sun

First printed in the music and alternatives magazine, *Planet*, 2nd June 1972.

By Paula Bellmaine (My name from my first marriage.)

I feel like putting a disclaimer in here: for the tone, and for some of the content. But I haven't.

I have taken two words out of the title above, the same two out of the body of the text, and changed one derogatory term.

Police Squeeze Communes

I'll assume that you're pissed off with something, call it capitalism, work, society, whichever you prefer. You want out.

There are three alternatives that I know of. You can live in a cave by yourself but unless your parents happened to be Tibetans you will probably go slowly mad with loneliness. You can become a lifetime traveller, thus evading responsibility for most of the mistakes that other people make around you. Or you can find some others who share your brand of desperation and set off to start a separate society of your own i.e. a commune. I ignored the first alternative. I travelled for three years, ending up refreshed but more lost to normal society than ever, and four months ago embarked joyously on the third road.

Word came down through Paddy's Market that someone in Queensland had broken up 140 acres into small farms, the whole to be a commune. You could buy your own bit of earth (yes, that is a peculiar concept), ranging in size from five to nineteen acres for one hundred dollars an acre. Two acres of communal land would be left in the middle for a hall and school etc., My little boy and I and two young male friends leapt into my battered Volkswagen with enough money for petrol each way and nothing else. We liked the owner of the land at once. We hastened to swap prejudices and he said all the right things. Organic farming, Vegetarianism, Healthy air, Astrology, Get out of the cities before the big ecological, financial and sociological crashes begin. He and his wife had left exciting work in Melbourne two years before and they and their farm were obviously thriving.

Tom drove us fifteen miles to look at the land. We could hardly see it because of the scrub and our misty eyes and said yes, of course, six acres please.

Back to Sydney for a dreary few weeks to save the bread.

Made it up here. And for the first month I was so amazed and exhilarated at my escape from the city that I floated around in a euphoric daze. I sat in the creek imagining other people's traffic jams, remembered how I'd had to work at mechanical jobs, leaving my child with others so that I could earn money. To see him brown and free up here. He now instinctively trusts men with long hair, is very open and friendly with them and consequently has lots of father figures. If I am busy someone else is always available for a rough game, a story or the ritual counting of dead frogs.

Back to the new reality. This involves the hardest and most elaborate work any of us have ever done. Strange to live twenty-five years and not know the basic procedures for growing food or building a house. For the first two months here, there was unseasonable drought. Carrying gallons of water from the creek up the slopes to our vegetable garden every day put a tremendous strain on our muscles for a while. Cities don't fit you for survival. The weirdest realization of all this came one night when I was in bed staring at the full moon one night. I found that I did not know what happened to it next. Whether there'd be a slightly smaller one or a new one or what the next night. Never mind. "The wilderness is calling back its children."

We find ourselves very dependent on each other. Having got away from being dependent on the great mass of human beings, we now find ourselves in a very tough, dangerous environment, so that while we've found a collective independence, we are even less individually independent than previously. Now we have to learn to share work, whatever material possessions we own, and the biggest test of all; the bloody washing up. Suddenly we're required to have a great deal more faith in each other than usual. The framework of this commune minimises those difficulties. In theory everyone can be involved in communal affairs as much or as little as they wish and stay firmly on their own plot the rest of the time.

This new way of being gets people even further on to the track of good health. It sometimes seems to me that the main topic of conversation around here is the endless comparison of one system of healthy eating against another. Living, eating and swimming naked puts a healthy glow on everyone's skin and is the beginning of freedom. It is good to be aware of being just an upright animal. You stay cool on the hottest day if you have no clothes on, the body being a very efficient air-conditioner unit of its own if it's not hampered. We have found a deserted beach fifteen miles away where we swim in the cleanest water I have seen since I was a child.

Nonetheless our personal liberation will take a long time.

Outsiders don't seem to think so. Inevitably when a local converses with us in the pub, his most insistent subject is 'free love' and they suspect us of all sorts of orgies that we're not uninhibited enough to enjoy.

Houses

We're having a bit of trouble with ours. We were a bit desperate to get away from the process of selling ourselves for money so we have virtually none to waste on building materials. We are trying to build out of timber and rocks that occur naturally on our land. Driving back from the beach the other day I saw another suburban-type monstrosity being built on a headland. Fancy face-bricks, enough room out the back for a few flowers, a tricycle and a Hills hoist. It wasn't the simplest box-type design and I estimate its 'value' at about twenty thousand dollars. A poor misguided family will spend the next thirty years of their lives paying for it. Paying for shelter! The second criterion for existence on this planet and capitalism has people convinced that it is right and proper that they should sell their labour, their energy, a huge whack of their lives, to PAY for it!

It might take four of us a month to build our house. This area has an extremely high rainfall. Our house must be waterproof. It must have sound guttering and good-sized tanks (second-hand, cemented) to collect the precious rain. One month's work. It can be as beautiful as we want. As simple or as complex as we need. How much trouble are you having with yours?

FIRE

The first three groups of us to settle here had to endure drought for the first couple of months. Snakes were coming out all over looking for water and the bush was paper-dry and whispering to be relieved and reabsorbed by fire. We talked about fire, dreamt about it, and arranged a distress signal of three hoots on a car horn. (When the fire came, the old VW was the only car in the valley and it did not have a horn.) We visited the forestry people for advice. They said they couldn't do anything. Too dangerous to burn firebreaks after August.

That very night Michelle and pregnant Lois came racing to our camp. Fire all right, on commune property and night falling. Half of us were in Brisbane that day. One car, pregnant Lois, two small children, three guys, and Michelle and I. We all raced to the creek to wet some sacks and then to the fire. It was monstrous and terrifying. We just stood, overwhelmed for a minute and then seventeen-year-old Bruce, country born and bred, took charge. Lois, the two kids and I piled into the car under urgent orders to get the fire brigade.

So we left the others there with no vehicle, all very excited and very inexperienced at firefighting. We drove madly to the nearest farm five miles away where we thought there might be a phone. There wasn't, but they are beautiful neighbours and they plonked Lois, who was nearly having a miscarriage by this, on a bed, provided the little boys with some distracting toys and the man agreed to get to a telephone so I could get back. By the time I got back, head spinning with anticipation, they had the fire almost out. They were filthy and exhausted and very satisfied. It took two hours for the fire brigade to come as there were three major fires in the district that night.

The fire brought everyone together more than anything else. There was suddenly a sense of being a village, a family. Communal meals became very frequent.

The Bust

Only a few days after the fire the most predictable and most threatening blow hit us. 8am. Heavy cops everywhere pushing sneaking elbowing terrifying with their swaggering leers. Caught us with thirteen marijuana seedlings in a seedbox right by our beds. Everyone else was clean. The cops gloatingly carted us off to gaol. There they used the usual intimidatory threats of physical violence and a very sordid one of threatening to take my little boy from me and make him a ward of state. After the magistrate had said we could leave on 1600 dollars bail, the cops used their own initiative and locked us all, including the child in filthy cells for six hours. Luckily a long-haired church minister heard about us and came and bailed us out. He makes a practice of doing that, for anyone. Ten days later we appeared in court, pleading guilty. When the magistrate asked us if we had anything to say we tried to tell him that he was just outlawing youth, that pot is good for you etc.,

    We had all sorts of academic studies with us that we thought he just may be interested in but he said that he refused to listen to any of that, nor would he hear our complaints about the way the police had treated us. 400 dollars fine or three months gaol each. 1200 dollars. Two months to pay. We should be buying water-pumps, cement, tanks, etc., Bruce doesn't think he can get the bread in time, he is only 17 and is earning 80 cents an hour slaving on a nearby farm. Roger is working until 3 am every morning, washing dishes in a big hotel on the coast so he should be all right. And I'm writing this in the hope of becoming a brilliant journalist overnight. Two weeks to go.

Queensland is very backward in its drug laws. The magistrate whom we appeared before raised the fine from 300 dollars minimum to 400 dollars that day. It seems that they've never heard of senate select committees or of experiments such as in Holland, or even of the lessening of penalties in some parts of the States.

Unfortunately most people convicted on drug charges seem to accept the treatment dished out by the cops, and the heavy fines. They seem to think that they'll just draw attention to themselves by taking a stand but unless we fight it, unless we use every means possible to convince other people that the drug is harmless and somehow convince magistrates that we're not entirely helpless, we are leaving them with a perfect weapon against us. They don't bust you just because you smoke grass, they often wait until you're a bit of a menace politically, or until they are sick of seeing your smiling face around.

Since the day the police arrived we have been besieged by health inspectors, reporters, photographers, tourists and dirty old men. The latter scare us. Bummer.

And so we come around, inevitably, to a social philosophy. All the earnest revolutionaries in the cities accuse us of opting out of our responsibility to stay and fight in the traditional manner. (Unfortunately it's usually a traditional sort of revolution they envisage.) That might be partly true if ours was the only commune. But it's not. The way things seem to be going there will be hundreds of them scattered all over Australia in five years time. I must grab this opportunity to see if we really can de-condition ourselves and to what extent it can be done for our generation. It may be far too late for us.

It is hard to learn to live without bosses and without the slotting of activities and the interminable escape offered by the rush of city life. You can't hide from yourself in the bush.

I need to find out whether human beings, given a healthy free environment can learn to live together peacefully. With love. Not just zap now we are all contented and loving, but using our imagination to deliberately change and experiment with our relationships with one another and with the outside world too. Do all that while learning to grow food and understand the seasons, and somehow teach our kids about biology, technology, ecology, music, psychedelic drugs, and everything else.

It is one possibility for survival.

Editor, The Planet:

Although this story was submitted on the same terms as any other, the Planeteers would like to urge that any spare bread you have could be sent to the commune above to help pay the fines.

They're not expecting it but if you send relief coins to,

Paula Bellmaine

1/21 Balgowlah Road,

FAIRLIGHT

NSW

they'll get the message.

Photo 6 Banana Shed, Yandina Commune 1971

Carlos, Roger, Me and Bruce.

Mullumbimby Dreaming

It is a well-known theory in psychology that a person's first remembered experiences form the emotional flavour of their whole life. Portia's earliest memory was of being wheeled in the pram by her Gran. It was raining, and she felt great, safe.

I first met Portia when she arrived in Cooper's Lane with her parents in their small flat-top truck. Mother and boyfriend it later transpired. Cool and practised hippies. Urban ones. The fame of the happening north coast must have spread. Portia was 11 then.

I remember their arrival both well and therapeutically. It was 1972.

Cooper's Lane was waiting. It was almost evening. The atmosphere was thick with expectation, though really I thought that I expected no-one. The waiting enmeshed within the smells of lantana and cow dung and of bush used to a high rain-fall. The landscape formed a small open valley, sheltered, fanciful.

Some palpable magic in the 60s and 70s caused the leap forward. There was Swami Compassion and all the others who taught that you can transform your mind and therefore the world. Baba Ram Dass. And the re-programming the bio-computer guy, Ken Keys. Theodore Rozak who said that we were moving towards a collective higher consciousness. Of course Koestler thought that we were mutating in *unfortunate* directions. And most of the scientists still say, and with such authority, that we are progressing marvellously towards nothingness.

I had only known one other landscape as poignant, as magic, its magic instantly apparent, and that other place where I could see reality shifting was a long way away – in Pakistan. It was travel that had first made me realise that you can break right out of how you think the world is. Break right out of yourself.

In both places, each morning's awakening would be exciting. What new wonderful thing will happen today? Who will I meet – connect with? What will I create? What good news will come in? What breakthroughs will be made? Into the high life again.

Portia's adults were friendly but self-possessed when they arrived in the smoky mists of Coopers Lane. They proceeded to unpack their flat-top truck. From Melbourne. It seemed a long way for the word to have spread. They probably rolled the first joint about then. It transpired that they had been camping and cooking lentils and vegetables all the way.

With the advent of Portia's mother Judy, the socialising quotient went up to total. I don't think that they were in their tent very long. One of the basic timber houses with the obligatory verandah came up and they were installed and forever welcoming of me and of anyone else so that there was a constant round of visitors from near and far. Always a joint, the biggest and strongest since the one that had nearly proved my undoing in Bombay. People could eat at their place too. Amid the constant talk.

I had somehow grown up thinking that socialising was occasional, (although I was good at it in high school), and that life should be mainly work and suffering. Here, in that house, and in that larger community, socialising came first. Often that meant there was no time for anything else. I have a vision of young women in long skirts, sarong or even sari style, not much fabric on top, floating around between pots of tea, Bushells and herbal, and joints.

Part of those visions may even have been before these three arrived but Judy didn't so much float as take over. She said that she thought she'd make a good brothel madam. I should have got her to extrapolate on that.

Portia's room was very basic and a bit dark and she hated it. The new life perhaps appealed less to her than it did to the adults or the younger children. As an eleven-year-old she was a bit unforthcoming and not too eager to please. Perhaps that was a strength.

Judy introduced me to fasting and used to give herself enemas in her garden. She said, often, 'it's only the body!'

Love One Another RIGHT NOW

Flashback to Sydney and to the First Commune
– in Queensland.

I was aware of being at a crossroads. The decision was in fact taken. In some romantic yearning part of me. I'd decided on the basis of what felt most honourably *me*. Philosophically *right*. I'd discussed it a bit with two of the young guys who hung around with me in the Stuff shop. They were 18 and 21 and I was 24, with my two-year-old son. God, I think the decision was finally made when one of them said something like 'your problem is that you don't want to embrace the counter culture life completely'. I was always susceptible to a dare.

The choice was opting out for the hippy life, the life we believed made more sense, *living* the revolution, or staying on in Moratorium politics. In the suffocating city.

Where I can see in hindsight, I already had some sort of a communal life. Mainly because of the shop, STUFF, that we had started as a centre for Moratorium activities in North Sydney and which I ran. It was a poster shop and the best poster was the one of the pretty young nun in the low-cut habit with Che Guevara's face tattooed on her cleavage.

My young husband who had travelled Australia and the world with me moved out about then and one of the young women from the group moved in to share the rent with me and 2-year-old Carlos. One of the men, a law student had kindly come with some tools and closed in a tiny verandah off my room so that I could put the child in there. When the shop was mooted as a centre for our anti-

Vietnam war work, I had said to him, 'I don't care what you pay me as long as it's the male rate. Pay me the lowest male rate not the highest female one'.

That scourge of women being paid less was just starting to be attended to in 1970-71. I could remember arguing the point with my mother when I was about 10 in the fifties. 'But man and lady bus conductors do the same work? And the ladies are paid less!' My mother answered that 'if there was any heavy work to be done, unsavoury customers to be dealt with, then the male conductor would have to do it'. In hindsight again, that couldn't work. Could it? There was surely only one conductor on each bus.

The law student was one of the straightest of us. So why did I ask him to the acid-taking party at the house in Cammeray when I already had my estranged but still loved husband coming and also the current boyfriend who was keen on a ménage a trois? (He was not keen on this with my husband but with another girlfriend he had.)

Life was complicated enough thank you very much. Probably to thank him for blocking in the verandah. At the party I kept running into him with a shock as I reeled between bathroom and bedroom and all the urges to be polite and a good hostess surged up, but each time I found myself wordless: dealing with the acid existentialism, the bedroom tentacles, and the moving bits of world.

We had named the shop *Stuff* and Julian painted the name and its whole front vivid and shiny with brilliant mythological figures on a bright yellow background.

Others from *Stuff* would call for us on Sunday mornings to go to the beach with them after my husband left us. They were mostly younger than me but they tried to help and I was thankful.

We had wonderful solidarity at demonstrations. At one at the football ground to protest the Springbok tour, we were outside the fence shouting out about Apartheid when the police lining the inside, tried to drag one of us over the fence. We held on to each other and they could not break us.

We instigated encounter groups at the shop as soon as I heard about the concept. I had done a year of psyche nursing immediately after leaving school. Before meeting Peter and starting the years of travel. The encounter groups were as good as acid for insight and changed perception.

There were several bright weeks with the sculptor who wanted the trois. He took me soaring on a motor-bike and was flatteringly attentive. We made love in a dip on a deserted beach in full sunshine. He said I was so beautiful with the backdrop of sand and sea that it must be my natural milieu and that he should paint me there. He didn't of course.

One night, after a stirring meeting in the Trades Hall in town, I stood outside at the end briefly. It might have been the night I made an impassioned speech about Vietnam which culminated in me being voted on to the NSW Moratorium committee. With the AICD: The Association for International Co-operation and Disarmament people and the union heavies. It was summer. I felt the combined warmth and intellectual endeavour of the filled hall as such a positive force and so encompassing of me that I wondered why I was leaving for the Queensland bush.

As wonder I might. That political togetherness in the *Stuff* shop and in town was perhaps as close to real community as I would ever find. But stronger ideals, and admit it *love*, had to be encompassed.

I already knew he was not for me. I'd tried it and to my great grief he had decided on someone younger and prettier. That was an issue when I was 25?

Jesse had changed his name from John Owens and had chosen to honour the black runner Jesse Owens. When I rang his place and asked for Jesse, his father would say 'I'll just call JOHN'. We'd spent just one weekend together. With many others. It was at the farmhouse on the outskirts of Sydney rented by Paul Delofski and friends – Angela was there, and Paul Joseph. A yoga and candle-making household. For a weekend of music and LSD.

Jesse and Paul Joseph played and sang together including their standard of the time 'Come on people, smile on your brother..... You've got to get together and LOVE ONE ANOTHER RIGHT NOW'. Someone was going to come and film them for TV the next day so Jesse decided not to indulge in the acid taking. I wasn't going to at first either so put it off for some hours which resulted in me being out of sync with everyone: with Jesse who was straight, and with the others who were at a completely different part of the trip.

What was most interesting to me is that an alarm was set for the morning. The acid-taking was to be early, probably to allow for recovery before the cameras arrived.

We all woke up, the rest of them took the stuff and then all tucked down in the sleeping bags for another hour's sleep! I thought that this was crazy. Knowing the extent of brain disorientation about to be caused I said 'but should you go back to sleep? You'll wake up and not know what's happening!'

But it was obviously of more concern to me than to them. I was very cautious in some ways, an anxious type. I remember being riveted with anxiety on a train back in the Broughton

Hall days when I was only seventeen. Possibly because I hadn't understood the coffee connection yet. That caution is probably one of the reasons I survived both those drugged days and the years of travel before them. Though I've never thought of it as a survival mechanism before.

It was lucky too that I had the child. He was with my mother for that weekend that I was at Paul Delofski's but I looked after myself far more once I had him, once I was even unknowingly pregnant with him actually. I lost the taste for alcohol one White Christmas in London. In the middle of a live-in party I suddenly thought *why* do we all drink so much? And stopped. So children, you started to keep me on the straight and narrow even then. And suddenly interested in the future and therefore in politics.

Anyway three years on in the outer Sydney farmhouse Jesse and I didn't manage to love one another in the sleeping bags on the floor. Some time the next day he washed his face and they made a good showing with singing and guitars for the Countdown TV camera.

The next week Jesse announced that he'd got it together with Trudi and that I should be happy for him, he was complete at last. It is a sign of me and of those times that I truly tried to be happy for him and mostly managed to. I played Richie Havens' 'Atonement', loving its depth of spiritual resonance and not knowing what I was atoning for.

But I was also hit with a double dose of grief – it was only months since my husband had left me and the two year old. I stayed at my mother's, not mentioning any of it to her, she couldn't be trusted with feelings, or to anyone else I think. My insides were wrung with pain. I'd come to a dead stop.

So, Jesse Owens had told me all about this land at Yandina, near Nambour in Queensland being sold off in shares by Tom and Kathy of Abraxus Farm, Mooloolah. Jesse wasn't going north for about a year till he'd saved enough money working on the roads. He was trained as a teacher but found the road work less ideologically trying.

It was to be probably the first commune of the modern era in Australia. Jesse suggested that I buy in too. I ended up going long before him, out of love for him although I knew he wasn't going to be with me. We shared a potent political vision. I liked his talk about being up against the barricades. That was the sexiest thing about him really. More so than the tight blond surfie ringlets and the lean body.

I'd at least share in his dream. Such can be the depth of yearning. And all the intellectual part about living the revolution – that I'd been dared on – all that applied too.

I lived there with the two-year old and a few others for a year. It was a very hard year. Police and vulnerability, snakes, fire, cyclone and floods.

We were the pioneers.

I left before Jesse arrived.

And yet, in Yandina there was sometimes the feeling that we'd dropped out of the world of strife. I remember thinking, among the sounds of the frogs and the running water, why is it always bad news on the radio? What about all the contented rural people in the world? Up till then the news had effectively mirrored my concerns. Suddenly I saw that it was the news of the racing-about men. Of competition and war and money and disaster. It was the first time I felt clearly a change of consciousness because of circumstance.

It was great to find there, that the fossicking at the dump served very adequately instead of the browsing and spending in shops that I'd always been so fond of. Carlos and I (and friends) lived on ten dollars a week.

But the situation was unforgivingly difficult. We were virtually camping in the dense and itchy Queensland bush. Chickens were left without food and water because I went away for a few days and forgot them. Some died and some flew out maddened with thirst when I rushed to rescue them.

There was strife with fellow communees.

How long can it take to water the garden and wash the clothes? When the only water is in the creek ten minutes walk down hill through heavy bush and then carrying water back up the hill. Just like in the 2/3rd world I suppose. It can take aaaaaallll the time.

And it was in Yandina that young Bruce talked lyrically of the soft rolling green hills of Mullumbimby:

MAY THE LONG TIME SUN SHINE UPON YOU
ALL LOVE SURROUND YOU
AND THE PURE LIGHT WITHIN YOU
GUIDE YOUR WAY HOME
(The Incredible String Band)
This became the song of the Nimbin Festival, The Aquarius Festival.

In Mullumbimby we stayed for some weeks in the Finn village which was a simple double row of unpainted timber houses huddling alone, up in the cloudy hills. Finnish workers must have arrived there years before, perhaps to work the cedar or the bananas and thought they'd build themselves a village. (Not realising what a difficult feat that is in Australia.)

I remember the first time I was driven up there: up a steep double track of concrete which finished in dirt and gravel. Then around the corner, and there were just ten or twelve houses in two approximate rows, facing each other. There was dusty clay-type gravel between them and long green grass all around with hints of some sort of purple flower which magnified the green through contrast. And further back but not far at all, there were the soft hills covered with lush green banana trees and curtained by mist.

To my city eyes it was amazing to find that people had wanted to set out houses to form a community. My experience had been that people had wanted to set out houses to preserve and accentuate separateness. Such greenness reminded me of the precious paint tins in primary school. We only got our hands into those on Wednesday afternoons. This was such a deep green landscape with suggestions of blue as had been in those paint tins. It was more a marine green than something I ever expected to see on land and it surrounded everything there.

I went into one of the houses. It was fine – it had just managed to miss out on fifty years of consumer-hype progress. Tina and friends lived there. Their bright coloured things were strewn around and there was a wonderful smell, 'Boronia oil,' said Tina. Through the window I noticed the begetter of the purple flowers: a jacaranda tree.

Now the village was inhabited by the *new* seekers after community. We'd come from everywhere: from the early communes further north, from England, from Australia's cities. Some had already been flower-children and some had just newly walked away from their so-far circumscribed lives. From jobs that meant nothing, and from jobs that took all their time – all their selves. From neighbourhoods where they knew no-one and from neighbourhoods where they'd always been known and that would not allow them to blossom.

Everything was 'faaar out'. I particularly liked '<u>faaar fucking out</u>'. It was our favourite expression meaning everything is so much more, so much better than before or than we could even have imagined. It was liberating too then, the new and bad language. I sat around in the Finn village crocheting with Tina, Marie, and Marie's sister Christin, and the others who came and went. We talked and passed constant joints, and I remember feeling very privileged.

Tina was my best friend in the early days up there and it was she who said 'I used to rush and worry about time until I came here and now I've got all the time in the world'. Like she reclaimed her life.

Tina's boy-friend – one of them – was an American G.I. straight out of the jungles of Vietnam who moved ceaselessly about, carting his cassette player and his stash everywhere. He'd arrive in one of the houses, turn on his up-to-the-minute music, light up and it was a party even if it was only 8 am.

It was funny he didn't mention Vietnam. His name was Ken. He had that, to me, very American knack of managing to make sex – you couldn't call it love and I reserved 'fuck' for expressions of astoundment of the far-out variety that couldn't be associated with this slight physical encounter – he achieved whatever it was anyhow without at any time making me feel desirable. Still, he'd also stepped out of the hurly burly: through the looking glass.

The hippy who was sub-letting the tiny house in the Finn

Village to me, wanted it back. It was really only a converted banana shed but perfectly adequate. There was even an old electric washing machine with an electric wringer above it, outside the back door. Superseded then, but only by about twenty years and a couple of improved designs. Things were not moving so incredibly fast then as they do now.

No-one had thought of planned obsolescence which was to prove such a travesty.

So I moved down to Cooper's Lane with the child. Into an unconverted banana shed across a creek. No power and just a water tank outside but I loved it. A couple of the houses there were still inhabited by banana farmers and the rest were rented out to the new people.

There was all day to look at the lush scenery. There was plenty of lantana and wild tobacco and camphor laurel too, but these things were not a worry to most of us new arrivals back then. In fact they were hardly recognisable as distinct species to our city-formed eyes which were struggling to learn new ways of focussing. It was just this generalised shimmering greenness and the pulsating Van Gogh sky and the humid buzz of insects.

There were big cows all around. I was chased by one once. I ducked round and round a car, thinking, but it's a girl-cow not a bull! losing energy with my squealing laughter and fear.

I loved the electricity-less dark and the quiet of the palpable night. The unknown. The new world. There were snakes, watch out! and wet feet from walking through creeks. After all the traffic and noise, the busy business of Sydney and Melbourne. After the appointments and delays, the pressure of being a cog in the city.

There was almost too much space and freedom. How to organise it? How to organise oneself in the midst of all this openness of time? This furry alive new world.

Instead of waking in the Lane Cove loft and facing a day with a young child and no other bonds: school and work but no closeness, no meaningfulness and no celebration; I now woke in Coopers Lane to the birds' chamber ensemble and the sighing creeks. It was often to the pouring rain too, but there was the high likelihood of kindred souls – we often got rained in together for days - of fun, of feeling part of a new, being-made community. Out of our own time, our own souls and hopes. Everything new. Was it like being reborn?

There was time for baking cakes. And endless drinking of herb tea. Some of the earliest deliberate manifestations of the new community were the full-moon dances and the market days at Nicky and Jane Shand's. One of the first currencies there was Mullumbimby honey.

Oh and I was learning about bees: from a straight farmer who wanted to share his knowledge. It didn't seem to impinge on Tom Mott as it did on most of the other locals that we were different. He was eccentric too so perhaps he just didn't notice anything funny about us. He taught me the ins and outs of bees and honey and he never put a hand or a word wrong.

Tom also shared his dam, at least with those who lived close by his place. You had to go down a little track, crowded with indeterminate growing things: ducking them, itching and breathing in the breathless inescapable pulsating heat. Then slip into the dam, made from a natural pool. It had a water-falling into it that you could float under in the inner tubes. The being in the cool water with the heavy splashing pouring in on top of you. And the sparkling blue dragonflies. Oh heaven.

And oh the adjustments. Most of us became sudden converts to vegetarianism because of lack of money, let alone ideals. No wonder we all got tropical ulcers considering the sudden change from too much protein to none.

And how much of the intensity, the magic, was because of dope? How much because of a new optimism? We had mustered one hundred thousand to sit down on Sydney's streets for Vietnam. And we could go bush, hormones breaking free into new realities: friends and love and closeness. Instead of the city and the suburban *separateness* of our former lives.

I made a skirt for the full-moon dances. We could feel the pulsing up to the time. We were outside so much that we couldn't avoid the messages from the moon. I was twenty-six. The skirt was translucent maroon over translucent turmeric yellow. Long and the maroon jagged all around the bottom edge. I had a little maroon top with mirrors from Afghanistan, short and obviously bra-less as it was only done up by a fastener at the top of the back, the rest of the back was open.

And we bathed in the creek where it pooled near the banana shed for a year. Winter is mild in Far Northern NSW but it still required a certain verve. I'd splash in, wash my hair and all over myself and dive back in. Carlos and I lived in the Shand's shed that didn't really close up and used candles and a little metho stove. I did feel there and then occasionally, that I could keep it looking quite nice. I'd never felt that anywhere before.

At first Preacher Barry was just another in the very social house where Portia and family and droppers-in lived. I could see that the others were a bit circumspect around him and quickly learned to be that way myself. He had a peculiar personality: speaking in a loud hawking voice as if to an unseen audience. He talked *about* the people currently present rather than *to* us. He *pronounced* and Judy, the madam of the house, winced.

This was pretty unusual. Judy was uninhibited and accepting of everybody. Too much so I sometimes thought. It sometimes felt like company at any cost. Some of them seemed what, time-wasters? Much too regular for far too many years with their dope-smoking. Not nearly enough brain cells left?

Preacher Barry was a different case. He ignored all social conventions. Like the autistic person though, he had special talents and his weren't to do with brilliance in numbers or science, his were to do with the frailty of others.

Preacher Barry had an impact on us all. He had the gift of naming where we were at or wished we were. What did he say? announce really, very loudly, always loudly to that crowded cafe at the Nimbin Festival when I was with my very new man. I was 27, and he, embarrassingly 21. 'There's Paula with her handsome new *young* man – she's always at the forefront of every new idea'. Or at the forefront of everything, something like that. And he was right – that was important to me. But in the ideas stakes, not about things like having a relationship with a younger man; that was just embarrassing.

Nimbin was best for me in the lead up to the Festival. Some of us went over there a week or two before to help with the setting up. Before the hordes. Before there were 6000 people in one field and a hearse full of drunks came and parked outside our tepee in the middle of the night. In the lead-up there was a woman about who was commonly referred to as the mad woman. Wild hair and all. She orated. She also chased someone's little four-year-old boy down the street shouting 'Kill! Kill!'

One day a couple of young guys were putting on a small show – poetry with music – in one of the town shops and we were quite an audience. The mad woman got up next to the scheduled (if I can use such a word for those free times) performers and although they continued with their act, she mimed her own dramatic statement alongside. So we watched two shows at once: the sort-of scheduled and the wholly spontaneous. It did seem to me doubly rich.

Photo 7 The Aquarius Festival, Nimbin 1973

*At the Nimbin Aquarius Festival.
Carlos Morrow and Sebastian Shand aged 4, far
left on stage.*

A Review of the movie *Kokoda* by Paula Morrow

2006

No of words:1413

Kokoda is a great movie. It's great because it tackles the difficult task of making art out of an Australian legend.

It confronts the big issue of fear in battle, the ancient terror of kill or be killed. It shows the despair of being very sick in a jungle that is dangerous in itself let alone with an invisible, bestial army hunting you.

The film tackles these big issues with integrity.

It is a low-budget movie. Grierson, the film's director said on ABC Radio National on the 1st May that it cost $4 million compared to about $100 million for the average American movie. To me that is good. It doesn't employ overseas 'stars'. That is also a good. I reject the wasting of money in the blockbuster era and I reject the confusing of acting (a great art) with celebrity (just money and fame and superficiality).

Kokoda begins with self-deprecating and especially each-other-deprecating humour, taking the piss. We quickly see that the men are missing everything: training, food, medicine, strategy and adequate leadership. What is worse, they have not volunteered for this. They are conscripts who are meant to be only unloading supplies and digging roads. The AIF soldiers called them, derisively, 'chocos', short for "chocolate soldiers", who would melt if faced with a fight.

From the start we know we are in for it. I knew I was in

for it before I went, of course. I avoid violence and horror in films.

It turned out that the trailers that came on before the movie were more horrifying to me. Especially the one about an ocean liner that is going to go down in horrifying, in your face, screaming drama.

I went to see the film because my father was on the *Kokoda* track, although he was in the AIF which mostly only arrives at the end of this film.

I nearly left 20 minutes into *Kokoda*. Then I thought, for my dad, whom I didn't know much, I will try and stay. I was clutching my bag ready to leave. I thought if the director pushes me this hard I can't stay. And then we realise that it was one of the soldiers having a dream.

A nightmare. I suppose this was a good way of saying metaphorically, this experience was a nightmare, from start to finish. It was for the New Guineans as well, and for the Japanese too.

One soldier sings a dry, humorous political song about their situation.

A small gripe about the look of the actors and it is probably just a lack of experience or a lack of direction; but there was something wrong especially in the first frames with the posture, with the look of the men. They looked 21st century to me, not 2nd World War diggers.

Is there a knowingness, including about being cannon fodder, that has seeped into our very faces and bodies now? Such modern or post-modern demeanour must be hard to put a finger on.

The AIF bloke who was shaving was an exception, and so, especially, was the officer at the end, played by William McInnes. I have noticed his chameleon abilities before, in Sea Change, and especially in the Robert Drew drama on ABC, called Shark Net, where I failed to recognise him for nearly the whole movie. In *Kokoda*, he sums up the war, and the track, and the 1940s by his brilliant portrayal of a sympathetic officer, through his posture, before he even opens his mouth.

I don't know about Shane Bourne though, perhaps he was picked for this role of cynic/doctor because he has played such a cynic in MDA. I suppose there was a rationale for having someone spell out that viewpoint. His best line was when they all upped and left him, with him saying 'Boys, no!' The amazing thing was that they WERE only boys. When will we ever learn?

Julie Rigg, ABC Radio National's movie critic, mentioned in a discussion with Grierson that the characters were not very delineated. I agree that it was confusing at first. There were a lot of characters and I could not work out who was who: who they were supposed to be with, where they were running to, or from. And I suppose that that is much what it is actually like, when you are in chaos in the jungle and the enemy is trying to encircle you and cut you off from retreat to safety. Not knowing where you are supposed to be, or where your mates are.

The surround-sound was eerie and evocatively successful in that I could hear gunshots and shouts from each side of the cinema as well as the main action in the front.

At the end of the movie I could really only name three characters. The relationship between the brothers was partly successful. Courage was shown in unexpected ways. The courage of Sam who does a Scott of the Antarctic, leaving the others so that they may survive longer. The courage of the younger brother Max trying hard, although thus probably signing his own death warrant, to send his brother off to save himself, without future guilt.

The fact that the 'toughest' guy who always wants to leave the injured and get on with it, breaks down at the end with the death of one of the trio who had been together right through, shows the emotional realism which makes up a large part of the integrity of the movie. Human beings are mostly partly brave and partly cowardly, occasionally up to putting themselves at risk for a friend, often too scared to even keep ourselves up to task, as shown by the hand shaking convulsively above the trigger.

Of course, the mind jumps to compare this movie with Gallipoli. And *Kokoda* compares well.

Gallipoli must have been relatively high-budget: I remember it as huge. I remember lots of close-ups of handsomely perfect young Australian men. It successfully debunked the idea of war being somehow justifiable and rational. It showed soldiers at the mercy of bad decisions higher up. But it idealised the Australian soldiers and mateship.

Kokoda's seems a more mature vantage point: showing the suffering and overwhelmed human beings.

And, like Gallipoli, it shows the sacrifice. Both movies show not only the sacrifice of precious young lives, a concept that I for one, grew up with a bit of a warped take on. I had the feeling that these young men 'Our Boys' had willingly at least to some extent 'sacrificed' themselves for our freedom. But now, of course, we know that others, especially generals and politicians, sacrificed them.

A man rang the radio show previously mentioned to say he was very upset by the film. He said it was supposed to show the bravery of the Aussie soldiers but showed them watching their mate being gutted and then beheaded by the Japanese soldier without them making a move to rescue him, 'when they had a Bren gun'. But that scene was I think, deliberately ambiguous. We didn't know how many Japs there were involved in that killing, and I got the impression that the process was too far gone when they came upon it anyway. And how terrifying for the onlookers! Portraying the enemy as bestial is a common ploy by governments and generals. Both sides are shown literally taking no prisoners in this film.

Some comfort is given to us finally with the speech delivered by the officer played by William McKinnes. He so movingly imparts sympathy and gratitude to them. He says he has never known better soldiers. They deserved that and more. I for one was very glad it was said. Recognition and appreciation, and the understanding that they had seen unspeakable horror is conveyed. The speech was the least that they deserved and takes us back to our idealisation of our soldiers and to the legend. It was chaos but it has great meaning for us now.

And in the night when I couldn't sleep, it was images of the movie about the ship going down, big-budget nonsense, adding nothing to our understanding of the world that kept me awake, struggling to make sense of meaninglessness. Most movies are just products, competing to grab our attention through gratuitous violence and horror.

The next day I thought all day of *Kokoda*, the movie, and how much it had given me.

Saving the figs, or not. 2011

First published in Radical Newcastle, an anthology of the History Department of the University of Newcastle. Editors: James Bennett, Nancy Cushing, Erik Eklund Published by NewSouth Publishing Sydney 2015

The efforts to save the figs from the vantage point of one of the arrestees.

Including in a light-hearted vein.

First published in *Radical Newcastle,* an anthology put out by the History Department of Newcastle University NSW and published by NewSouth.

The anthology was dedicated to Ben Morrow and Pete Gray.

Tues 10th Oct 11 Went into fig protest again today. Just 7.30 -9.00 am lovely loose protest. A few stalwarts but mostly people just wander in for half an hour or a few, and leave again.

2.11.11

From the agony to the ecstasy. That's what I felt after hearing later, in the police station, that the fig trees, had minimal if any damage! Bryce had sent Justine a text. Before that I had felt, Oh No! So much effort and we are losing them anyway. After that I was just thrilled and stayed thrilled for 24 hours. The sense of accomplishment......So unusual in the protest movement to get instant results. Or any.

I felt despair as the chainsaws and the big crane revved

up. And the crowd in Laman St, concentrating on telling the police to 'wait for the injunction', did not seem to notice that the chainsaws had actually started. So I decided to jump down from the tree and run towards the centre, towards the machinery to try and alert the crowd. Knowing I would only get about two feet. Two or three cops grabbed me, I was upset, shaking, saying to them, 'there'll be none of nature left', 'there'll be no atmosphere for the kids to breathe'. They nod. A young one says 'will we let her go?' And the cop in charge looks me in the eye and says, 'No, arrest her, she's trouble!' And I think, Yes, I am too.

It had been a big day. I got there about 5.05 am. Woke at 4 thinking 'the trees!' a bit before the 4.35 am I had set the alarm for. As I walked into the park, the street lights were weird with the dawn light increasing as well, and there was the unusual addition of tents! In the city park where a few protesters had slept the night.

I see Lynn, Pete Gray's mum arrive. She is, like me, the mother of a champion activist. Both of these beautiful young men have died of cancer over the last couple of years.

One of the organising people, whom I know and trust, tells us that there are attempts to get an injunction to stop the carnage, but that the chances are slim.

The birdsong is wonderful, special, poignant. It may be the last day of their sonata in this spectacular canopy of fig trees in the heart of our city. I send a text to local ABC radio, 'U should hear the bird song in the Laman St figs.' And sign my name. It was then 5.23 am according to the message still on my mobile phone now.

And it was only about an hour after arriving, that a few people pushed a fence panel over and got in. I hadn't even considered whether I was going to try and get in. I was just here to protest outside the fences. But as I got near the area, I felt the old excitement rising. The panel was hastily put up again by the security guards. Young J ran up behind me and said 'do you want me to take the fence down again'. 'Yes!' says I and 'Are you coming in too?'

He takes it down and I am in. But he doesn't follow. Three other young people do. I don't know them and they seem unsure of themselves. And then we are in no-man's land between the two fences, I say to them, 'We are in!' and they say unhappily, 'Yes but it is no good! We can't get any further'. I look around and yes it is true and slightly embarrassing to be there, caught between two fences, in no-man's land, between two worlds. For the first time that day I think of the Berlin wall. Although really, in Australia, they don't usually shoot protesters.

The young people go back but I wait by the second fence, wait for an opportunity. I am experienced and can bear being there alone and obvious for a bit. I try and get between the security men who are moving between joins in the second fence but the guards don't let me. And then one does! Maybe he was embarrassed too or perhaps he is on-side. I am in!

I see another activist I know and we do a bit of a jump around victory and hug. He had disabled the fencing which is why it was able to be lifted off. I know him from the anti-coal protests. And the protesters' café.

There are about 12 of us within the two fences now and some quickly climb trees or chain themselves to poles. I say to someone 'The security guards didn't really try to stop us!' and she says 'No they don't want to'. And I remember being briefed another day that if a security guard touches anyone, they are required by law to follow it up all the way to court. I think now too that some of them have been very kind to us through the whole stand-off. They have been hanging around the coming and going community of people trying to save the trees for weeks now.

And the guards have had to be there all night. With the trees. I felt that the couple of nights I spent in the Tasmanian forests allowed those forests to imprint on me. A lot of the security guards are probably sympatico with the trees by now.

I give a leg up to a woman I know who is trying to climb into a tree. I am moving around a bit, having a few words with each of those others now inside two security fences with me. The fellow who pulled the bolts reminds me it may be the trees' last day. I take a few photos of them in the early morning light.

I get a text from my daughter who I knew was aiming to get down to the protest about six am, saying that about ten people are supposed to be inside the fences. So at 6.34 am, I send one back to her saying 'I am one of them! Am down near the Dawson St end. x o x o'

She replies that she will come around to that end. I see her in her corporate work gear with her bike in the crowd and it feels strange to be talking to her through two wire fences. There are about thirty people up this end now, and I hear it is the same at the Darby St end, and I can see quite a few down in the park as well. I tell my daughter that it reminds me of the Berlin wall and remind her that a friend of ours was in Berlin on a student exchange when the wall came down.

Someone is taking coffee orders! I have never had this luxury in a sit-in before. I tell someone that Ben and the other direct-action activists didn't and don't get that. And Ben was a coffee enthusiast. These are inner-city trees! Amid the civilised delights. If we can't save these few special figs, how on earth can we save the forests, save the planet?

My daughter who just has an hour or two to protest on her way to work, gets involved in buying the coffees. About eight coffees and a few bottles of water are passed to friendly security guards and then over to us, inside. Some guards will do this, and some will not. It becomes obvious over the day that some are on side with us or at least humane enough to pass food over, and rubbish out, and some are not.

My daughter then goes off to move my car out of the two-hour parking zone for me. The day looks like being long and will probably end in the police station. I start ringing patients to re-schedule them. My political interests have gone against my work ones many times in my life.

And then my daughter has to unlock her bike and go to work. 'Love you Mum', she says through the fences, 'Love you too', say I. Feeling life and its dangers and fleetingness, just a little more poignantly than usual. It is not a dangerous situation. But I have given up my relative freedom for the day.

I am not a physically very brave person. Not like those young ones who live in platforms so high up in the trees, or hang off the cables of the coal loading machine in Newcastle Harbour, or lock on to moving machinery in Bayswater Power station. Who all, like me, believe that there is little time to warn people that Mother Earth is being killed.

The woman I helped up into the tree wants to leave and go to work! So I help her down. I decide to climb up into it. It is only about one metre up into the fork of the huge branches. It is very cool there, although out in the sun the heat is threatening. The bark of the tree is actually cold. I put my face against it.

I take more photos on my phone, including of myself up there and send it out to the local ABC (who I never hear back from – journos now often have a very different idea to mine of what is the news) with the subject line 'up a tree in Laman St', and to family and friends. I ditch the first couple of me looking glum with my glasses on. And take one with my glasses off and smiling into the camera. How relaxed do we have to be feeling for vanity to clock in? Pretty relaxed.

I start talking to the guy in the next tree and take a photo of him. He would be over fifty too. He is up about a metre higher than me in a much more comfortable position: he can sit and move around. I am standing wedged with my feet in only a couple of possible awkward positions. We have a laugh that he is able to have a coffee, a ciggie, and is reading the paper, just like at home. Later, on the ground for a while, I read the paper too, but only the fig-tree related bits; concentration for other news is a bit low.

It becomes a rather peaceful few hours. I try to keep an eye on Anne who is older and who had got herself tied to a post with a bike chain and was just sitting on the gutter. We at least got her up on to a chair and a hat on her. And Norm in his eighties, our most amazing protester of the day, has a chair in the shade.

People donate us a chocolate cake and a lovely big variety of salads from somewhere, 'from a sympathiser'.

A bloke in the crowd who has a slouch hat on and might be a farmer quietly grabs the opportunity when a guard is handing rubbish out, to get him to pass a hand of bananas in for us.

I hear later that as well as the vociferous groups at each end of the enclosed area, forty people are sitting on the floor in the council administration building, chanting 'don't cut before the injunction'.

It was deeply satisfying to feel that I helped.

It seems that I see a breached fence as a great opportunity! That says a bit about me, I suppose, but a lot about the state of the world.

Oh Newcastle! Oh Planet! a poem

By Paula Morrow

The Cutting Down of the Laman Street Fig Trees Newcastle, 2012

That was a terrible symbolic act, the destruction of those fig trees.
If we can't save a few beautiful trees,
in a stunningly beautiful street like that,
in the middle of a big city like this...

When so MANY people cared so MUCH!
Including little children

How can we ever save the planet?

The people with the power don't understand the basics
about how to keep a biosphere going.
About ethics.

They don't seem to know that trees make oxygen!

They didn't get up close and touch those magnificent huge limbs.
They weren't there at 5 am to hear the huge range
of blithe birds in their dawn chorus.

They didn't understand that the trees were spiritual beings.

How is it that we have people taking our money,
who know nothing about the important things?

Nothing about ecology: how every living thing is connected.
Nothing about the biosphere:
that small fragile layer on the surface of the earth.
Green and brown. Blue and invisible air.

We depend on it utterly
As do all other living things spinning with us through space.

The spoilers and the wreckers get the power!
Ignorance and machismo is winning.

Lots of us are exhausted.

And most of us did nothing
'Worrying about our mortgage and our silly little phones'
Great line Paul Spencer!

And some of us who did, could have done more.
Some good people even at the table, tried
Until it was too hard
The difficulties hit our families, our ordinary lives

Soon there will be no ordinary lives

Shades of The Ancient Mariner

And the Indian Chief
'When will they find they can't eat money?'

We can't give up on our use of oil, and coal
But this is the Solar Generation, elsewhere
We have the best solar capacity in the world.

It will only begin to change
If most people start to do something

Spend 10% of our time, making those in power
do what needs to be done, says Paul Ehrlich

Up against the immense wealth of the mining companies
And the lobbyists for greed
With their media connections

Socialism is still not to be mentioned

Why can't we have the best of both
worlds?
It might be Social Democracy,
like Scandinavia?

The free market is devouring the planet.

The Joy of Protest   2015

This was up on the *Radical Newcastle* website for the year after the anthology was published.

I just told a bloke I met for the first time today in 'Suspension', the most activist-friendly coffee-shop in Newcastle, that being involved with groups that protest, that work for positive change, is enlivening.

I am here to tell you that you feel extremely alive when you paddle a kayak out on to the harbour with many others as part of one of the 'flotillas' organised by Rising Tide and stop the coal ships for the day. Vera Deacon did this in her eighties!

It reminds me of the day 100,000 of us sat down in Sydney's main streets for the Vietnam Moratorium. And stopped the city.

And when you trespass on to the coal loaders and stop them operating for a few hours.

Or when you run breathless with fear and excitement (and probably lack of fitness once you are over fifty) through the fence and up on to the mountains of coal in the grounds of one of NSW's filthiest power stations, 'Bayswater' near Muswellbrook. You feel very alive then.

I have form as an active member of the Vietnam Moratorium. I was voted on to the NSW co-ordinating committee of the Moratorium, at the age of 24 when I was single mum with a two-year-old, or a 'deserted wife' as they called us in 1970.

I arrived in Newcastle in 1988 with three of my four kids, 15 months after my second husband died of cancer. We were following the eldest who was starting university here. I straight away looked for groups similar to those I had been involved with on the far north coast of NSW: environment groups and Quakers.

I went to some environmental group meetings which spawned Newcastle Greens and also Trees in Newcastle. I was one of the earliest in Newcastle Greens. And later on I was the (un-official) Newcastle representative to the Greens' meeting in Sydney that made the decision to form The Australian Greens. I just said that I didn't think that Newcastle Greens would stand in the way of such a move. (That being the low level of enthusiasm I had judged from our group, for centralisation of any kind.)

My three younger kids were exposed to people talking about politics. I especially remember one magical Greens' night at John and Carrie's that included as well as big pots of food, someone playing the didgeridoo. I was glad that they experienced that particular night. This was about the time that Ian who was one of the organisers of The Wilderness Society Newcastle, came on board with the Newcastle Greens and that felt like a strengthening. (I had joined The Wilderness Society from the far north coast, soon after it was formed over the Franklin River crisis.)

Other environmental groups started springing up about ten years later, notably Rising Tide. I have been arrested three or four times over the past four or five years with them. On the coal-loaders twice, in the grounds of Bayswater power-station, and in the entrance of parliament house, Canberra. I must come across as a middle-aged feral!

I am happy to answer to the term environmental activist. Or to hippy, from my positive experiences in the hippy commune movement from 1970 in south eastern Queensland and in far northern NSW.

The *Sydney Morning Herald* was recently kind enough to call me an 'eco-writer'.

April 08 trespassing on the site of the 3rd coal loader.

The only time I got arrested with my full-time forest activist son Ben was on the first coal-loader jaunt. He had already been diagnosed with cancer by then, had had the exploratory surgery that could do nothing, and a few rounds of chemotherapy, but bounced back into his old spiritual self with the leadership qualities he had exhibited when he came into his own in the forests of NSW and Tasmania.

I felt constricted with fear for him. He was taking photos. It was raining and cold and muddy. Later we were all, about 23 of us, held and harassed in the police station cells in Newcastle for hours. They had taken our water bottles. There was a tap attached to the top of the filthy toilet in the cell I was in with four of the young women. None of us drank from it. I was concerned about Ben, in with the other activist blokes, but weakened by illness and treatment. In the cells with the idealistic young women, including one who meditated for a bit, I started to tell the story of being in the police station in Kuwait, when I was twenty and a traveller, and how much more desperate and dangerous it was then. I think it was Naomi who particularly wanted to hear, but we were interrupted by the police wanting to catalogue us: photos and fingerprints.

I was concerned that one of the young women in another cell, Chrissie, might get hypothermia and told a cop who seemed to be interested in OH & S and he went and talked to her and got her a blanket. You can always rely on those people, and the reps in a place, to take some responsibility.

The police took everything: our jewellery, wallets, and the

aforesaid water bottles as well as our fingerprints and photos.

At one stage an assertive and cranky female cop asked us if we wanted her to get some Maccas in. It must have been about 2 pm by then. I was more concerned about us not drinking anything for hours. All we protesters and ferals had strong ideas on nutrition too. Young rangy men started saying 'Can they leave the meat off mine?', and 'Can I just have chips?'

'If you are going to be pedantic, I won't bother!' said she, and she didn't.

Pete Gray had told us early in the day, at our six am start, that he was not happy missing out on actually being in the protest. I assumed he was on bail or something. Pete had a whole feast lovingly arranged for when we got out, late in the day. He had a table set up on the path right outside the police station with a huge selection of breads and dips!

There is often this intense appreciation of each other as individuals who have bothered to step off the well-trodden path and put ourselves on the line in order to try and wake the population up. Wake up to the dangers of evaporating our coal-mines into our atmosphere. Our grandchildren's only atmosphere.

Bob Brown said at Ben's funeral in Newcastle in 2009, 'He was one of the VERY FEW WHO ACTUALLY GET IT!'

Before that I tried to get arrested in the same vicinity as Ben was trying to not get arrested. I walked into the exclusion zone of the Weld Forest in Tassie earlier in 2007. Ben and other direct action activists were climbing through the bush secretly, so that the police could not grab them and put them out of action, while lots of us were walking on the easier logging road. It was still seven kilometres each way, deliberately in the exclusion zone. Including young women with prams. There was a young bloke on crutches who told me he was just going to go as far as he could. On that stony logging road. There was a public and media blackout zone so the logging company could take out more old-growth forest. I had meant to get arrested but they did not arrest any of us that day. I showed the cop on the boundary my roughly-written sign as I walked in. It said 'Mother Earth is Dying'. He said 'I know, I am just working here'.

I have written about meeting some of the Tasmanian forests through Ben's inviting my daughter and me down there in my novel based on truth: *Darwin's Dilemma: the damage done and the battle for the forests.*

In November 2008 we trespassed on Bayswater power station near Muswellbrook.

It was a big drive. I took my car. Jude sat next to me. Jonathan aged 20-something in the back said something about the despair of having all this environmental catastrophe on us. And I said, No! It was ever thus! Before we knew all this. It is the existential angst! The anguish of being conscious beings in animal bodies. I certainly felt it as a young person very keenly, extremely keenly, reading Albert Camus. Fromm was the antidote, *The Art of Loving* shared amongst those of us who most needed it. And then later *Island* by Aldous Huxley. The impetus for my own utopian novel, *Life in Time*. Jude later said that she enjoyed that conversation between Jonathan and I.

Graeme Dunstan was there in his very obvious van. It had a loudspeaker on it! I knew him vaguely as one of the organisers of the Nimbin Aquarius Festival in 1973: the *'Survival Festival'*. I went over ten days early from my banana shed in Mullumbimby to help with the setting up of the festival. Graeme made us a cup of tea out the back of his van after the Bayswater escapade.

I felt again the rush of fear and excitement as we breached the wire fence. And then we run, together. Get in before they stop us! As usual I giggle with the excitement and the unusual effort and wonder if I will keep up. Later, further in, the black mountains of coal are huge and the coal slips away from under my feet which makes me giggle more.

Later we covered for the couple of photographers who needed to get out and get the film out.

One of the workers said he thought we were doing the right thing.

When the police were there and we were reduced to lots of standing around on top of a hill, one of the young protesters said that he thought it was like the anti-Vietnam protesters, everyone thought they were wrong at first and then they were proved right. He seemed a bit thrilled when I told him that I had been part of that too when I was about his age. I was even voted on to the organising committee of the NSW Vietnam Moratorium when I was 24.

And the only time I have been arrested with my daughter was in 2009, in the entrance to Parliament House Canberra, with Rising Tide and people from other states. About 200 of us were arrested when we gathered to try to encourage Kevin Rudd to go for reasonable targets at Copenhagen. My daughter had been radicalised when we spent the night in the Styx Forest as guests of Ben and his small band.

Mind you, I also feel very alive when I swim in the sea, or walk in the bush, and surprisingly when I catch public transport. It takes me back to being a kid, when we all walked or caught buses or trains a whole lot more. A bit of discomfort (not too much thanks!) activates the senses. As does the witnessing of human interactions when we are out in the public space, as opposed to sealed, de-humidified and homogenised, in our cars.

How much more do we then feel enlivened if we meet with others of similar values and try to push for environmental sustainability, or for social justice? And get out there in it?

As Pete Gray signed off on one of his emails to a group of us fellow protesters,

'Pleasure makin' trouble with you!'

Photo 8 The Florentine, Tasmania 2007

Paula, Ben and Abigail Morrow, The Florentine, Tasmania. Ben died of cancer in 2009. Photo by Allana Beltran.

Broughton Hall 1963 - Flashback

I hadn't realised that I was so lucky to have the nervous breakdown I did, when I did…

It was at the end of 1963, a year that had consisted of 1st year Psychiatric Nursing, starting on the 30th January that year, my 17th birthday. At North Ryde Admission Centre, the new, state-of-the-art Psychiatric Hospital in Sydney.

The minimum starting age for psyche nursing should have been 27, not 17, in retrospect.

It was a year of hard knowledge, hard drinking and 'pep pills' - amphetamines - taken to stay awake on night duty or the commonly-demanded 16-hour double shifts.

The pills then also taken because they worked well too, to stay awake and ahead of the game when talking philosophy and drinking alcohol at the pub, especially The Royal George, in 'Town'.

But then, my best friend, co-nurse and unofficial tutor in philosophy, Simone, four years older than me, was leaving to go back overseas. (She is mentioned in my first novel, *Life In Time*.)

I went to sleep at the wheel of my little red Sprite (bought on 50 pounds take-over terms, loaned by my grandfather, and without a reverse gear), one morning after night duty and crashed it and more of my dreams.

I had delay action shock and depression, and withdrawal from the uppers: even hearing voices once (fears of schizophrenia!) and landed in Broughton Hall. This was a voluntary and free psychiatric unit for disturbed young people in an old building set in beautiful gardens with streams, huge goldfish and little bridges! It was on the periphery of the beautiful grounds of Callan Park.

There was a great young psychiatrist, Bob Gordon, who took an interest in me. He gave me almost daily Freudian full-on analysis: that is being drawn out, encouraged to free-associate, and listened to, with only occasionally, a little feedback where my attitudes or beliefs were particularly self-destructive.

'But WHY would you want to believe in Free Love?'

I have hearkened back over the years to something else he said which probably has wide relevance to all of us:

'The psychological theory is that we have the emotional predisposition first, and then find the philosophical and political belief systems that tie in with that.'

He also gave me the full gamut of IQ and personality tests and lots of group therapy which was the new thing then and which I had experienced and been impressed by, when working at North Ryde.

He later gave me LSD intravenously – it was mixed luck - this latter. He said he was interested in my IQ and my desire to write, and that the experience might help my creativity.

There was a vibrant patient body!!!! We had our own group conversations going endlessly, sitting in small groups out in the sumptuous gardens under the trees.

'Cured neurotics are the salt of the earth', said Syd, a very handsome older man. What, about 23 years old? So he was intelligent too. I was still 17.

A few of us recommended books to one another – I remember Erich Fromm's *The Art of Loving* (I still would recommend it) and RD Laing (not so sure). But we also hopped out to the Orange

Grove Hotel, fell in love with one another, and popped out to a motel, or down to the storage sheds which smelt of the tarpaulins which could become makeshift beds.

The pills Dr Gordon tried on me caused major problems. They dropped my white blood cell count dangerously low. He took me off them, was perturbed and didn't try me on any others.

It was some time soon after the couple of months in Broughton Hall, that I realised the connection between coffee and anxiety in me and became more careful with that.

I was standing on a train in Sydney, with the first big love of my life, Peter, and was suddenly gripped with severe anxiety. I thought 'but nothing's happened!' Wondered what was different and realised we had just had a real coffee. Coffee shops were still rare then but we had been to one, in 'Town'.

I'd been out of Broughton Hall a few months, I may have still been attending the Outpatient Clinic occasionally, but I doubt it. Peter's sister Julie told me decades later, how sophisticated she thought I was, saying sometimes, 'I just have to ring my psychiatrist' and popping into the nearest public phone.

We had all had our small jars or tins of instant International Roast or similar in the nurses' home at North Ryde, Simone introduced me to that too. There were the large tins or jars for coffee breaks in the tea rooms on the wards. Coffee with milk and two sugars. And the constant cigarettes! Looking back, it wasn't much of a jump up to the stay-awake pills: the amphetamines.

But it was the real stuff, the espresso in the rare European-styled coffee shops, that packed the punch and among the good feelings, raised the anxiety levels.

It had always been just tea from the teapot at home.

***

Although I remember Broughton Hall fondly, of course I was partly trained by then and some part of me was sweating blood, wondering what my being there meant for my future.

"Cringin'!" as my son Jesse would say much later as a teenager. Or "Spewin'!"

As it was, I was discharged with a diagnosis of anxiety disorder, after a reverse group meeting with just me and a few doctors/therapists.

We can be masters of our own fate by seeking out and following up on therapeutic groups, knowledge and proven alternative health as well, while still keeping up with the wisest orthodox medical advice.

I now know that people need to be extremely careful with alcohol and any other drugs or medicines, both recreational and prescribed.

Moods, Food Cravings, Addictions: notes for workshop August 2017

Paula Morrow, Naturopath, Herbalist, Clinical Nutritionist, Author

We should not eat anything or take anything that is stronger than us or where there seems to be danger of addiction.

We live in an addictive society, including with gambling, shopping and on-line activities. Of course, every marketing person wants their product to be addictive. And now, the way things are going with increased competition, just about everybody needs to market themselves.

Blood sugar needs to be addressed and can be a direct cause of mood swings and encourage addictive behaviour.

A high nutrient, low GI eating pattern needs to be taught around the individual's preferred foods, with as wide a variety of health foods included as possible: healthy proteins, plenty of vegetables, with a reduction in sugar and white flour products.

Supplements that help mood, stress and blood sugar. The basics are Chromium, Vitamin B complex, or preferably a multi with the Bs in the correct ratio to each other.

Magnesium: There are so many on the market but only a couple that I recommend. You need top brands for absorption.

Omega 3 fatty acids for brain function.

We know that alcohol doesn't work as an anti-depressant – it is actually a depressant! but it is a very good anti-anxiety drug – there is a better legal herbal one available recently.

I am trained in Western Herbal Medicine, Acupuncture,

Naturopathy and Clinical Nutrition. So European herbs plus American Indian Herbs. With the best of Chinese and Ayurvedic herbs added on to our knowledge over the last couple of decades.

I am particularly impressed when a herb that has a long history of traditional use keeps coming up now in the scientific literature….. and for the same usages as the traditional. To me this is about as good as it can be: the marriage of science and folklore.

The latest very potent anti-anxiety herb is not from any of these traditions and is knocking our socks off with its fast-acting effectiveness.

The other major anti-anxiety herb is from the Ayurvedic tradition and is wonderful too, but is more of a long-acting one. Not the half-hour turnaround of the previously mentioned herb.

These and the major anti-depressant drug, European, need to be prescribed by a practitioner who knows what they are doing because they can react with other commonly used medical drugs.

We need to understand some of the dynamics of addiction/ craving especially food/alcohol/drugs/medical drugs….. Don't just take yourself off anything medical without proper advice….

There are extremely good herbs but you need a consultation to determine the right herb or combination for you.

Stress connection: how to keep it down with exercise, relaxation, laughter, the right sort of social groups for you.

Nutrition totally affects the mind.

Psychology help is available.

Groups: company versus isolation

Of course, we don't have to take all the herbs, vitamins and minerals etc., all the time but rotate them as we need to. I try to teach people who come to me for consultations or workshops to do that too.

And now, from my lifetime of work as a natural therapist, as well as a writer, I know the best anti-anxiety herbs and mineral supplements to have with coffee if necessary!

Three Elders and a Television Set.

The tube went on the old tv in the middle of a cold Saturday afternoon when I was watching an iconic movie, *The Company You Keep* with a visiting friend Julie. Wine, bikkies and dip, the lot and then poof the main entertainment gone!

I had another old fat tele in the back room but how to get it halfway up the house to the antenna connection with just me and my friend who is recovering from a broken shoulder.

Having a rest, looking at the sky, lying there thinking it needs to go on wheels, what do I have on wheels that would be strong enough, the shopping trolley is not strong enough, nor are any luggage things, of which I have a few!

I know, the office chair, it must be strong enough – the old TV, although heavy, couldn't be as heavy as a human being. OK but we have to wait for N, male housemate also over 60, skinny vegan, does that matter, to come home.

I make a bit of a diagram of where I take out the plugs that connect the DVD player to the broken TV. Where it is black words on black I can't see the letters and Julie holds a torch for me in broad daylight. As we look for clues on the back of the old unit, she points out that some of them have been grouped together with a white box shape around them, I wouldn't have even noticed that by myself.

I feel a bit despondent when I notice that the input plugs on the new (old) TV are configured quite differently, are even on different sides of the set! Would not even be attempting this except that I saw a young female friend setting all this up very confidently recently.

N gets home smiling and relaxed, and we pounce. He can lift

the replacement TV, no trouble, on to the wheeled chair. I mainly just have to steady it (lucky that son-in-law mentioned last week that all the weight is in the front of these old TVs – we act on that and face the heavy side to the chair back) and N and I manage to wheel it down two rooms and he can lift it up next to the non-functioning one.

N is moving the old tele out of the way along the sideboard and I can see the cords that connect it to the set-top box and outside aerial being seriously stretched, I am saying 'No, No, the connections!' and Julie is saying 'We told you to disconnect it! Didn't you disconnect it?' she yells at me. N is looking unhappy and I have completely lost the words to shout, 'No not these ones, they are still joined up!' N goes off to his room in a light huff, he hasn't even had time to take his jacket off before we begged for help.

When they leave me alone for a minute, I find that I had indeed disconnected some things, power from the wall – old conditioning – but not others.

I rescue the over-stretched things, muttering about breaking cables, and think I will have one stab at re-connecting to the new one, otherwise we will give up until someone young and tech-savvy will be here on Monday, two days off.

I connect them up and it works! Not only that but it is a much better picture. Hooray!

Back to not only the exciting chase story of Robert Redford and other great actors young and old, but to the romance of being involved in Save the World activism.

I was saying to the small group of friends: PH JS and RS, that I heard Andrew Denton interviewing Peter Singer, the Australian philosopher and animal rights writer on the radio once. Andrew said, slightly querulously for Andrew 'Do you mean we can't have meat at all Peter?' And Peter slightly acerbic as usual said 'You can eat road kill Andrew!'

As we were laughing about this, probably more so because it was in a slightly unfortunate social situation for the topic, a vegan café, J spluttered, 'I thought you meant Andrew was going to go out looking for road kill then and there'.

'What in Paddington!' says I.

'Hunting and gathering!' says someone.

'You'd need an accomplice! 'I say, giving a bit of an inexpert soccer-type kick into air, and thinking of all the poor over-civilised moggies and dogs around Sydney.

The Arrest! What is a conservationist these days?

And who should be going to court? For crimes against humanity.

OR It was a long way to go without a swim.

Over the last few months I had put up the idea on face book a couple of times, probably on *Lock the Gate*, why not converge up there this winter, envisaging you know, mid-July, when it is coldest down south and hopefully lots of retired people with a little bit of cash or credit and a lot of sense, might choose to put themselves where it could help against Adani's proposed giant new coal-mine for a week or so. True eco-tourism. So then when it came up and FLAC (Frontline Action on Coal) were calling for people, I felt well I HAVE to go.

Even though winter had gone in September when I heard the call and went up to face Adani and the police. And long gone when I went back there to face court in October.

The magistrate at Bowen court in Nth Queensland asked if we, the four of ten defendants facing him that day on the charge of trespass on Adani land last month had also managed to be involved in the cleaning up of the wetlands which apparently had been happening at about the same time nearby!

I was concerned that he was accusing us of hypocrisy if we didn't do both. He could have no idea of the effort involved for each of us to converge up there.

He also said when reading someone's references, 'your actions are not out of character, it's your character that makes you take them', perhaps taking issue with the writer of the reference. This showed more depth of thought and possibly therefore understanding, than I was used to from magistrates.

So I thought that I would tell you a bit about the sort of people, especially the majority of them who are young to very young who are involving themselves in these actions.

First off, they/we think we are taking desperate, rearguard action to save the planet. To wake the majority of people up. To put our minds, a lot of our time, and if necessary, our bodies on the line.

Because we think Earth is at, or fast approaching a number of tipping points from which it may not recover even to the extent, I fear, of agriculture being viable for continued human existence. Let alone our children and grandchildren inheriting a beautiful green and blue planet on which to live out their lives and expect to be there for their offspring. An expectation that all humanity has had so far.

The Adani mine being started in Central North Queensland is at a nexus of time and place.

Just when the world is waking up to the damage we are doing by evaporating our coalmines into our atmosphere, our government can't resist the urge for yet one last quick lot of bucks, one last fix. And is prepared to subsidise to the max, that is, give one billion dollars of taxpayers' money for Adani to build a railroad between his mine and his port.

This means devastation to the Barrier Reef from accelerating climate change, and also poses an immediate threat to the Reef as ships laden with coal sail directly over and around it!

And they are to be given unlimited free access to precious ground-water!

We were arrested for trespass when deliberately standing across and blocking the Adani-owned road into the Adani-leased Abbot Point Port.

I see a lot of these young people making enormous sacrifices: deciding against a normal career or having children.

A young woman I met in Tasmania on a walk-in trying to save one of the Tassie forests and who was a friend of my direct-action activist son Ben said to me that she was an artist and her parents would have liked her to finish her last year at art school but she thought that so much more of the Tassie old-growth forests would be felled in that year if she stayed in college, and she pulled out in favour of protest action.

And hypocrites? Another very young woman I met in Tasmania said to me that she felt awful that women had to use more toilet paper than blokes. How intimately these forest activists see our over-use of paper, made out of their beloved forests.

Six weeks ago, on Friday 15th September I caught the train for the nearly 3 hour trip to Sydney and stayed with old friends who have a B n B in Enmore. I nearly cried when the taxi arrived at 5.10 am the next morning instead of the 5.15 I had ordered him for, and I jerkily threw the last couple of things into my bags. It was dark and it is hard on me to get up very early. It was a short trip with a kind and trustworthy young black taxi-driver.

It turns out that there is another protester on the plane, dressed like an up-market bushwalker, very schmick walking boots, only one empty seat from me, and she says there is another woman further back. We two talk excitedly for a bit. She has a family and a business and is originally from Bulgaria, we discuss the wisdoms Europe lately manifests.

Off at Proserpine (Whitsundays) Airport and the third woman meets up with us at baggage collection. We are expecting a lift and as the people thin out, we walk out into the sunshine just as a young woman jumps out of a car and comes over to us. She looks at us expectantly, 'Stop Adani!' I say, half exclamation, half question. 'Yes!' says she.

A frisson of excitement runs through us all. It has begun.

I settle down into landscape and the memory of landscape for the one hour drive. It is such a long time since I was driving north into North Queensland. I am looking for the sugarcane and there is some but it is just young shoots.

When you are older or have had a lot of loss or change, or education even, maybe, you are living all the time with a lot of layers, a lot of resonances. That really hit me going north, going to Queensland again. First with Peter, hitchhiking in big trucks, we were 18 and North Queensland was shimmering sugarcane and love. But there was also the beer-drinking with the truck drivers at the rest stops. Travelling back in time 53 years ago! But that person is always within me, as in all these flashbacks, movies, of my mind.

The third woman off the plane is in conversation with the animated English-sounding young driver and it appears that the passenger and her partner back home have been living for the past few years in Tasmania, only fairly recently left there, where they created and worked a sustainable small mixed farm. She must be capable of hard work. We will all turn out to be people of high endeavour.

When the four of us roll up into the camp which has been named Babirra meaning Echidna, there is some loud squawking as a flock of black cockatoos fly low overhead and settle in bushes not far away! Black cockatoos only appear very rarely in inner-city Newcastle, and then always singly. And on the gate, I get a hug from N, a young woman I have known in Newie for years as a fellow activist and whom I admire.

There are a few simple rooms and a couple of shared bathrooms and some covered areas surrounded by camping grounds. I am pleased to find I have a mattress on a floor in a small basic room. I am obviously sharing with some male whose shoes are in the middle of the floor. (I have indicated to the organisers beforehand that I don't think I can carry a tent all that way. Filling in difficult on-line questionnaires.)

AND 4 steps from 'my' room, in a central under-cover area open at each end, is a table with a cheap electric jug, a few mugs and some instant coffee and tea bags!

I am a bit concerned when they say that they are all drinking bore water but soon find a very large rain water tank, not far from the tea station. And try to tell everyone to use only that in the jug. I don't know how much notice is taken of me but then a sticker appears on the jug from its owner saying please use only rain water in it as otherwise sediment builds up in the jug. As a health worker I am more concerned about sediment building up inside us.

It is interesting but difficult over the next few days. It is very well organised and there are constant meetings. Two young people volunteer to produce three vegan meals per day and they are prepared with very generous vibes. With love, actually.

We are 120 strangers who have interrupted our busy lives and travelled here out of conviction. As in any group there are conflicting emotions of inclusiveness and lording it over others.

We visit a close-by beach walking along at evening with our beautiful banners after a talk by an indigenous woman elder. There are a lot of huge tree limbs as driftwood that I assume to be part of a cyclone some time ago. A couple of media people are there.

And the next morning we gather with banners on another beautiful Whitsunday Beach, and hear from indigenous elders of the area. Their knowledge is so precious. They have to trust us now, there is no-one else to trust.

We have come all this way because we think it is vital for the Barrier Reef, for our planet, and for the coming generations, that this mega-mine not be built.

Ten of us volunteer to be the arrestable ones at the first action. It is at an after-dinner meeting in the big marquee-like area joined on to the built-area of the camp. One of us is to step down later saying that maybe she should avoid being arrested as it will be awkward for her business. I think ruefully, one thing getting arrested never is, is convenient. It has never been good for my very small business.

We stand together in a separate group and I feel a sort of silence come over us.

I feel the same way in the sleeping bag on the mattress on the floor that night. A quietness of the decision-taken. The action is to be no big heroic deal, no climbing, or arguing with machinery or courageous acts like that, but it is a line crossed: in intention today and soon in fact.

The next day was more meetings in the morning, a bit of a blur. I have started missing some of them and I know by now the other people who dislike them too. One young woman arrives from Melbourne and tells me she has decided not to go to any meetings at all! She has come especially for another action planned for later in the week, that I know nothing about. So there is secrecy and stratification, perhaps necessarily so…

We spend the afternoon doing role plays on a dirt track next to the camp. Four times we go through what we are going to do the next day. I have never had rehearsals like this before. Have talked processes out before but not acted them out. It is hot and the gravel is hurting through my sandals. I decide to wear my 'good' shoes tomorrow because they offer a bit of support and protection. They might get wrecked but I know from past experience that it is better to wreck shoes than feet.

I decide I had better search out and finally find, a Red Cross patch, just a red cross painted on to a square of calico, that I was supposed to collect a couple of days before, because I am one of the few with First Aid training. Those and other cloth badges have been lovingly made by people there. I pin it on to the back of my shirt.

I had put up my hand for volunteers who are practised in counselling too. So I am supposed to have a Welfare cloth badge as well. But when the 'Welfare' group started meeting for an hour at 7 am, meeting just with other 'Welfare' volunteers before the main meetings of the day, I found that too hilarious and said I don't think so.

I was having trouble with the corporation-like organisation including endless meetings that were a bit too structured and not inclusive enough for me, that is, not drawing out the inspiration and experience of each individual. The few other long-term protesters around seemed to feel the same. It did end up helping with efficiency, but perhaps lost a bit of the larrikin energy and fierce protection of each other, of previous incarnations of the movement.

But there was a lovely woman in that welfare group who listened to me about my concerns at one stage, about us not putting the reef up on our banners and material, risking not making clear enough why here and now is such a special space and time. Young Hannah listened too when I complained about the sort of corporate-style management. Very generously in her case because she had been acting as our leader, given too much authority, therefore diminishing grass-roots democracy. Without those couple of instances of being heard, I would have perhaps gone home prematurely.

What I am saying I suppose, is that FLAC represented a new style of group for good (lots of) and bad ... to do with less grassroots democracy (and is possibly only my perception). The previous anti-coal group I had often been arrested with, first called Rising Tide and then other titles, was driven by individual activists being more spontaneous.

The day of the 'action' dawned cloudy, thank goodness! I had been wondering how long I would be able to stand up to the heat out in the open. Breakfast was all ready for us even earlier than usual, about 6 am.

We knew which cars we were getting into for the short drive to the Adani-owned private road. We had sorted all that out the day before. There is now talk that police may be up at the end of the private road into the camp and some worry that we may be stopped by random drug tests before we even get to the highway.

At the last moment when I am sitting in the front passenger seat, we need a new driver for the jeep we are in and I say 'well I can, if I am good enough! Just an ordinary NSW licence?' And I swap seats. For the first few minutes over the bumpy dirt track, I feel my nervous excitement about to go through the roof but then I think, this is nothing, I have driven semi-trailers! (*A very long time ago, at age 18, when hitching around Australia: exhausted truck drivers having a nap or at least a break from their amphetamine and other speed based journey*).

Once I get the knack of getting my foot up high enough for the brake pedal in the jeep, it is all good. Slightly hairy before that, foot searching desperately for the brake as the jeep heads a bit too fast down into a half metre ditch in the sandy dirt road.

Note to self later: when driving a new car, feel for the brake pedal before you drive off.

There are no police waiting and we turn off in convoy on to the main road with a sigh of relief.

It is only about 15 minutes along the highway, me trying to get the others to talk. *Sharing a previous long-time ago time that I was arrested in Queensland. 47 years ago.* Trying to make the others feel better.

I am driving blind, not having been a designated driver yesterday, I wasn't privy to where exactly we are going. But very soon, we see the bus we are following veer off to the left and follow them and stop.

Hoping my stamina will last! I had a respiratory virus before leaving home, actually had to miss the first plane I booked and lose the money, because I was not well enough, and have felt deaf in my left ear since the flight. And I have had dreadful up and down blood sugar since I was a small child.

It's quickly out of the vehicle and as soon as there's a break in the traffic, across the road and down the private road, walking fast, running a bit. Then holding hands, we turn around and block the road. The aim is to let no more workers in that day. It is about 8.30 or 9 am.

We hold up a huge colourful banner, 'Reef Jobs NOT Coal Jobs'. At last a message succinct enough for me, mentioning the reef. There are about 40 of us across the road. A very cranky cop drives right up to us shouting that he will arrest all of us if we don't let him through. The other younger Paula and I find ourselves right in the middle of the front line. He stops the car just before our knees.

I look past Paula along the line to Anna and Elle and say 'We only agreed to block workers, not police?' (I find out later that this cop is trying to escort a worker in). Nobody answers me.

I say 'OK then', and turn back firm to face the cop, thinking this action will be over very quickly if we deliberately block police and that he will force us backwards with his car against our legs.

But then the good young guy from our group who has volunteered to be police negotiator steps up and defuses things.

Quite a lot of media is turning up, looking wide-awake and interested.

We take the risk of moving a few metres further into the private road where it will be much harder for cars to get around us. We arrange ourselves the same way facing the entrance from the highway in two rows, with our big banner of iridescent fish and coral. Those of us who will defy orders to depart and therefore be up for arrest, are still part of the front line, with another line of protestors behind us. About 40 or 50 of us in the two lines and as many others, around in various back-up roles.

A couple of police-people negotiators arrive, very relaxed and chilled and the atmosphere cools. And we stand there, chanting, Stop, Stop, Stop Adani. And sing good songs. Including We Will, We Will, STOP YOU and Coral Not Coal. And hold up our great banner.

And Graeme Dunstan who has made the banner brings two beautiful slim vertical banners on bamboo poles, each of a black cockatoo. And for a while we hold one of these up on each side of our main banner. There is some muttering in our front row, that our 'Reef Jobs NOT Coal Jobs' is too strong a message, upsetting to locals employed in the coal industry. I say if that banner goes, I go. Thinking if you think we are here, to not threaten coal jobs, you are a bit naïve.

The media troupe is growing satisfyingly and feels somehow on our side. Microphones are stuck in the faces of a few of us intermittently, when that happens to me, I dredge up my strength and say something about the habitat for our children and grandchildren and end up with 'Wake up Turnbull! Wake up Shorten!'. A woman standing behind the interviewer nods and smiles at me, indicating 'that was good' which is a help.

Next time I might say 'Wake up Governments!' because some of this stuff ends up going around the world.

We got the word a bit before this, that the police are already in, that they got there before us. And about now we turn around to face them. They are lined up further in, across the road like us and about 100 metres away, and they look a bit threatening. The riot police with pants tucked into boots and weapons. Grim with the dull sky behind them.

Our line can relax a bit as we have swapped around and are now behind the protestors who have been holding our backs. We now are holding theirs. I even manage to send a photo of the riot police lined up against us as a text to my daughter. A lucky breather as I realise that I am tired already. The line of comrades now in front of us hold up their sign made of separate letters to face the police line. They spell out: WE WILL STOP ADANI.

We have more standoff and singing for about half an hour.

Then a woman representing the Adani company steps forward and officially asks us to leave. We won't, and then there are similar statements from police. Those of us who have committed, prepare to be arrested. We were back to nine at the beginning of the day, but a young woman from the general group of us still spread across the road decides that she can be arrestable too and so we are ten again. A little boost to us nine. The ten of us sit down. What makes you up for arrest when crunch-time comes, is refusing to move on when individually ordered to do so.

So the police move up to us as a line. They have no idea whether we will resist arrest or whether they might have to drag or carry us. We are sitting in the gravel. We have decided days ago not to make them carry us. We certainly won't resist arrest, that is a higher charge. As a policeperson taps each of us officially on the shoulder and asks us will we move and we say 'No', they say 'You are under arrest' and we get up and go with them. I am about the second to be tapped and I get to my feet between a young female cop and young male.

You can feel their relief. We are going quietly. I am glad that that part is over too as I am led to one of the several paddy wagons waiting. I say to the two guarding me and a few other young police behind them 'I hope some of you agree with us! Especially if you have children!' And it registers in their eyes. I think they mostly do agree. I have been told that that is the case with the cops in Newcastle.

They ask me my basic ID, and I ask the woman cop her name too, thinking they are supposed to tell me.

'Natasha Marshall' says the woman with a smile. We are behind the wagon now and the media can't see us. Both sides of us have fronts to keep up!

'Natasha! Nice', I say. Me being of the Dr Zhivago movie generation. 'Did they bring you all from a long way away? We heard that some of you were brought in for miles.' I probably sound a bit apologetic about people having to get up very early.

'Oh', she says, 'we don't mind! We see friends in this team that we don't see otherwise. We'll, you know, catch up with them for a coffee later'.

The two cops go through my bag by the side of the paddy wagon. They need to know everything that is in it and then put it in a small storage compartment, away from me. That takes about another 15 minutes and then I am glad to slump on to the narrow metal seat in the wagon.

It wasn't such a shock to the system for me to be arrested as it was to many of the others because I have been arrested against coal before, a few times here in Newcastle or the wider Hunter Region over the last thirteen years (and once for the city's trees). And once at Parliament House, Canberra.

But this time being in the paddy wagon and then a cell for a few hours brought back vividly the first time I was arrested in Newcastle with a lot of young people including my son Ben who was a forest activist in Tassie and who had been diagnosed by then with the cancer that was to kill him in under two years. So I was having flashbacks to our beautiful Ben, both in the paddy wagon and in the cell.

I sometimes think that I have lived a life of so much un-processed grief that it comes out and grabs me at unexpected times of resonance.

As they processed each of us into paddy wagons, they kept

opening the door to see if we had enough air. A, another older woman who was put in the wagon with me, said she was cheered to see me so relaxed when it was such a new experience for her. But I was just exhausted and thinking of Ben.

Back at the station and they took me in to the processing room first, they must have been concerned about my age. There is always a bit of apprehension, I had been treated badly by police when very young, and seen others treated much worse, including recently. But over the decades of political correctness (political soundness the very philosophical crime writer, Reginald Hill calls it!) police have mostly improved.

At least I thought we were all progressing, even if of course unevenly, in the English-speaking world, until Abbott and Trump and until Brexit.

A cop who would have been in his forties welcomed me in! dismissed my escort in from the wagon about two metres away and said in a very friendly and soothing sort of way, 'Hello Paula, I'm Craig and this is …' introducing a young policewoman as I step inside too. They couldn't have been nicer even if the policewoman did have to stand and sort of obliquely watch when I asked to use the toilet.

They took my hand-made red cross badge – more good organising, protesters' camp – off the back of my shirt (I had only found little gold safety pins to pin it on with) and unpeeled the Stop Adani badge from the front. I had to hand over my jewellery: rings and earrings all totally sentimental including the one my Mum had had made for me out of my Grandma's tiny diamonds back when I had my first baby in London.

And the earrings Ben brought me from Rajasthan, worn thin

from too much wearing. The police were reassuring as I made sure I could see each piece in the plastic bag, checking the earrings twice, and my debit card, purse, phone.

I could take nothing unnecessary into the cell. I said 'Hey my asthma puffer is in my makeup purse, I don't get asthma often but when I do, I need it, I might get it under stress'. Craig said 'Are you feeling stressed now?' I check internally, it is still mainly relief. 'No' say I, thinking this is all slightly humorous. He says 'if you get asthma, how long do you have to get to your puffer?' I think and say ten minutes.

He says 'see that's all right then, we'll keep it safe for you'.

And then they ask me answers to a long questionnaire about my mental health and my mental health history. Obviously to suss out whether I am a danger to myself with anything left on me. And they put me in the cell.

A bit different to way back in the Vietnam Moratorium days when the NSW Premier, Bob Askin, when asked to comment on the protesters, said 'Run over the bastards!'

And of course you always notice the ugliness of the cells: they are meant to be a deterrent! The walls are painted in gloss paint and there is graffiti. You would have to be seriously thirsty before you drank out of the bubbler sort of tap on the top of the toilet in the very bare cell. There were two concrete low bunks, just flat steps off the floor, with grey plastic covered flat cushions that could be spread out to make a thin mattress and the stainless-steel toilet combo in the corner. ...I register the harshness but I still feel relief. I put a couple of flat cushions on top of each other and sink down on them.

It is only about 20 or 30 minutes later that H is brought in with me. If we are 10 people aged from 20 to 71 as the local paper reports the next day, then H is one of the two aged about 20 and I am the eldest. It is lovely to see her. Such energy! Instead of just sinking down she does a few yoga poses, including what looks too hard to me, lying backwards on the high, sloping down concrete half-wall that forms a part-screen in front of the toilet.

H had felt claustrophobic in the very small space in the paddy wagon (they divide them into four different sections in Queensland ones) and told the police checking on her that she had to get out. I am very interested in her story that comes out over the next few hours, as gradually the other women are brought in and we are eight women sitting in there, being quite jocular.

H has gone to a very expensive girls' school, that a young woman in my adopted extended family also went to. H said it didn't particularly go with any sense of entitlement from her home. Her parents worked very hard to afford it. She had done some university, to do with social justice areas, including aboriginal studies. Very committed to all forms of social justice. She said, 'I am so glad I didn't end up in some big job'.

There is something about that statement that makes me feel that I must remember and repeat it to my high-achieving daughter, honorary niece and daughter-in-law.

At one stage, I start yawning non-stop and say to the other women, 'my blood sugar is dropping'. They ask the police, they must have pressed the button for help, and ask if I can have a cup of tea. 'Yes, milk? how many sugars?' someone asks. 'One', I say. Craig appears with a styro-foam cup pretty soon. 'Oh thanks Craig!' I say.

'Oh, you are on first name terms!' say the women.

I say 'He introduced himself and the young policewoman to me as soon as I was brought in!' I had assumed he did the same for all of them.

Craig says 'Sorry I can't make you all one, haven't the staff.' And seems to mean it.

So much for all my fears of red-neck police from so many years ago in Queensland, aged 24. Those sort of policeman (we never saw a policewoman back then) are long gone. As is the 24 yr old woman I was, or is she?

And I am maybe more able to see police as human beings since I have been reading Reginald Hill compulsively for the last couple of years. A writer of huge philosophical and writerly talents who wrote, among other things, the Dalziel and Pascoe novels.

We are finally let out one by one, about 4 pm: back out through the processing room where we are reunited with our stuff. The young policewoman now on in there, says 'it's not often we hear "thank you" in this room', and the blokes concur.

We find that a couple of comrades from the camp have been waiting down in the waiting area of the police-station since we were arrested in case we need a lift back. That is a lovely feeling. They too, have gone without lunch, in case we need them.

'But you could have walked up to the corner and got yourselves something to eat!' I say.

Freedom! That very lucky state of affairs that most of us take so much for granted in this country. And autonomy! The latter may be the most jealously guarded attribute that humans have.

We head back to the camp. When I left it long ago this morning, the site seemed a bit bare, scrubby, no big trees, like a lot of the Australian bush.

When I got back after a day of strain though! When I got back to the camp it was like paradise. Vibrant, colourful, full of good people whose values I shared, they clapped each of us who had been arrested that day into our eating area under the marquee and after dinner presented us each with a big Bowen mango! I always feel a slight frisson at the first mango of the season and this was a presentation one!

So that was how it happened, getting arrested against Adani in September 2017.

I was very glad that an interesting photo was taken of me being arrested, taken by Alex Bainbridge whom I had recognised at the camp in the first day or two, and re-introduced myself to. We had both a few years back run for parliament in Newcastle, me for the Greens and Alex for the Socialist Alliance. The picture showed older woman being led off between two police, and got up fairly widely on the social, and maybe the mainstream media.

It was exactly that sort of picture, on the teve as my first husband Peter used to call it, that gripped my, and many other people's imagination in the Franklin River campaign long before. I particularly remember one guy, of grandfather age, sitting head down on the river bank, huge heavy machinery poised behind him, being pulled to his feet by two policeman and walked away between them. To be immediately replaced by another silent peaceful protester: by a great long line of people, older mostly, ready near the river! And we kept seeing more people every night on the tele; they filled the paddy wagons, and presumably the cells, in front of our eyes!

The other momentous images of the long-ago past for me, were the immobilised, oil-drenched dead, or worse, sad, birds and sea life of the till then pristine-seeming ocean when the oil

ship Exxon Valdez in 1989 struck a reef and went down. You can google the images.

According to a steward's announcement on the plane, it took 15 tonnes of fuel for the return trip Sydney to Bowen. I don't usually want to be so greatly increasing my emissions by flying. I heard this on the second trip in two months. Back to face court.

It was a long way to go without a swim!

We defendants, and our lovely female pro bono barrister, had a bit of a giggle before court about the need to call the magistrate 'Your Honour' and not to call him 'Your Majesty' by mistake, as my daughter and I so loved in the movie *'Gettin' Square'*. The barrister replied that she has had defendants do just that, and even one who called him 'Your Honour, Mate'.

Chat with Eva, the shuttle-car driver in Bowen   2017

There was a recent Sunday evening activists' get-together, where I was asked about my two recent trips to Bowen, firstly to block the workers and police on the Adani-owned-road to the Adani-owned-port and get arrested for it, and secondly to go to court up there.

Ian asked what I had said to the woman who drove me in the shuttle car on the one-hour trip from Proserpine Airport to Bowen, that she told me had converted her in just that time.

CHAT BETWEEN EVA WHO WAS DRIVING THE SHUTTLE CAR AND THE PROTESTER ON THE ONE HOUR TRIP FROM PROSERPINE AIRPORT TO BOWEN, OCTOBER 2017.

What I said to Eva the driver, who had kindly offered to take my backpack out to her car, while I waited for my bag on the carousel and who was then really angry with me when I came out and got in the front seat next to her, because the small backpack she carried for me, had a 'Stop Adani!' sticker on it.

I said that I really didn't want to argue about it while she was driving, that I was exhausted from travelling for 24 hrs (had not had much sleep in the YHA dorm in Sydney on the way), that it would have been better for me in every way to have not come: because I had to cancel some of the regular babysitting that I do for my grandchildren to support my kids to work, that I had a big writing deadline coming up that was put under stress by me taking off up here for the second time in two months, that I was neglecting my Natural Therapy work.

(Thinking that I generally was wishing I was not up there being told off by her, but softly, softly, because I was so tired.)

She told me after ten minutes chat that I was a nice lady, but that people like me had no right to come up there and spoil the chances of work and money for their town, that population and house prices had gone down in the past year. She said it was because of uncertainty about the mine which they had thought seemed a sure thing.

I said that this is a very special place and time. Right between the proposed new Adani coal mine and the Barrier Reef. That the huge Adani mine will indirectly affect the Barrier Reef (and the planet) through increased climate change, and directly endanger the Reef by being shipped from here with the damage of spills.

That I was only there because I think that the planet is in dire trouble: that I wouldn't have come unless the situation was looking desperate for the next generations. That I am already very stretched at home. That these two trips and the fine are coming out of my very dwindling house deposit.

That the web of life is very susceptible to damage, that we are on various tipping points now. That if we disturb our ecology (the green and the blue and the soil layer, and our thin band of atmosphere) much more, the next generations may not only lose our beautiful, workable climate, but that agriculture may become impossible.

And yes that I get her worry about the population of Bowen going down from 10,000 to 8,000 and house prices dropping, and that I will try and spread the word that Bowen needs futuristic jobs, but that I refuse to believe that people want jobs that will destroy their children's world, their chance of a liveable planet.

Photo 9 Police across road, anti-Adani arrests 2017

Image ABC Police line blocking us on the Adani Rd, Bowen before the arrest.

Photo 10 Outside court after appearing Oct 2017

I am in the middle. Court after the Adani arrest.

Photo 11 Carlos's 50th birthday 2018

Carlos, Abigail, Jesse, Claudia and Paula Morrow.
(also on backcover)

Other books by Paula Morrow

Healing Ourselves and Our Earth: The real health insurance and the diary of a natural therapist.

Life In Time is a novel with a slight speculative fiction device and is loosely based on the author's early commune experiences.

Darwin's Dilemma: the damage done and the battle for the forests. This novel has two themes. One follows a small band of activists sleeping in trees to block logging. The other focuses on a group of uni friends trying to unravel a vital mystery. Did Charles Darwin actually say what he is reputed to have said... and how much does it matter?

You can contact the author at:

paulamorrowauthor@gmail.com
https://facebook.com/paula.morrow.399
or through her website at https://paulamorrow.net

Wishing luck and love to us all.

Wishing luck and love to us all